Introduction to Literature

English 1

Third Edition

Janice Campbell

Everyday Education
Making time for things that matter.
www.EverydayEducation.com • www.DoingWhatMatters.com

Excellence in Literature: Reading and Writing through the Classics

— **Introduction to Literature (English I)**

— Literature and Composition (English II)

— American Literature: A Survey Course (English III)

— British Literature: A Survey Course (English IV)

— World Literature: A Survey Course (English V)

— The Complete Curriculum (All 5 years in a binder)

Third Edition: © 2014 Everyday Education, LLC

Second printing 2017

Everyday Education, LLC

P. O. Box 549

Ashland, VA 23005

www.Everyday-Education.com

Front Cover Art: *Jerusalem Pilgrims* by William Strutt, 1872

Campbell, Janice

Introduction to literature / Excellence in literature: reading and writing through the classics / Janice Campbell

ISBN: 978-1-61322-039-9 (Perfect bound)

ISBN: 978-1-61322-023-8 (Coil binding)

ISBN: 978-1-61322-025-2 (E-book)

1. Literature—Explication. 2. Literature—History and Criticism. 3. Books and reading. I. Title.

It is a great thing to start life with a small number of

really good books

which are your very own.

You may not appreciate them at first.

You may pine for your novel of crude and unadulterated adventure.

You may, and will, give it the preference when you can.

But the dull days come, and the rainy days come,

and always you are driven to fill up the chinks of your reading

with the worthy books which wait so patiently for your notice.

And then suddenly, on a day which marks an epoch in your life,

you understand the difference.

You see, like a flash, how the one stands for nothing,

and the other for literature.

From that day onwards you may return to your crudities,

but at least you do so with some

standard of comparison in your mind.

You can never be the same as you were before.

Then gradually the good thing becomes more dear to you;

it builds itself up with your growing mind;

it becomes a part of your better self, and so,

at last, you can look, as I do now, at the old covers

and love them for all that they have meant in the past.

—Arthur Conan Doyle, *Through the Magic Door*

Thank you!

I would like to offer special thanks to some of my former students,

who graciously agreed to share their work as models.

Erin Bensing

Jonathan Bensing

Eric Lansing

Rebecca Shealy-Houghton

Jesse Thompson

I would also like to thank

Rebecca Shealy-Houghton- Research Assistant and Website Editor

Craig Campbell- Music and Historical Context Consultant

Maria Gerber- IEW Project Manager

Deo gratias.

Contents

Introduction

Dear Student,

Do you know that very few people know how to read?

It is not that they cannot decipher words on a page, but they simply do not know how to place what they read into its proper literary and historical context. They may understand WHAT happened in a story, but they do not know WHY. They may feel strongly about the story, yet they never stop to wonder WHY they feel as they do, or HOW the author made it happen.

If you are wondering why you should care about the HOW and WHY of literature, think about it like this: Reading without understanding is like walking onto a softball field and batting the ball, without any knowledge of what to do next. You may hit the ball out of the park, but if you do not run the bases and complete the play, you have missed the whole point of the activity.

It is the same with reading. In order to complete the process, it is necessary to think deeply about what you read. Reading is a conversation between a reader and a writer. The author creates a world, peoples it with characters, and presents a story. The reader enters the author's world, meets the characters, and follows the story line. When you write about literature, as you will this year, the conversation shifts. It becomes a dialogue between you, as an analytical reader and writer, and the reader of your essay.

In this literature curriculum, I will introduce you to a technique I call "deep reading." As you work through each assigned story, you will also learn about the historic, literary, and artistic context in which the story was written. I will give you the opportunity and resources to discover more about the story, the author, and the various elements of the text, including plot, setting, characterization, and more. This will help you make sense of each great book and will make the story more enjoyable.

You will find that you like some books and authors better than others, just as I do. Each novel, poem, essay, or play in this literature series has been carefully chosen for its quality and its place in the panorama of literary history. Even if you find you do not enjoy a particular work as much as another, it has been included because it has something important to convey. One thing you will discover is that sometimes the stories you like least stick with you the longest and sometimes even teach you the most.

I love to read, and I am happy to have the opportunity to share some of my favorite great books with you. Some will make you laugh, others may make you cry, but above all, I hope they make you think. When you finish your reading for the year, I know your mind will be more richly furnished than when you began, and that is a very good thing.

Janice Campbell

www.ExcellenceInLiterature.com

P. S. As you read through this book, you will most likely encounter words you do not know. I am sure you know what to do when this happens. Look it up and write down the word and its definition, and you will be expanding your vocabulary without much effort at all.

Overview and Objectives

Excellence in Literature (EIL) is a college-preparatory course of study. It is my goal to

- Introduce students to great literature from the Western literary tradition.
- Teach students to read with discernment.
- Train independent, self-motivated learners.
- Provide tools students can use to strengthen their writing skills.
- Introduce students to sources for high-quality online and off-line research.
- Prepare students for college classes by expecting carefully researched, well-considered material to be presented in standard format, with preliminary proof-reading completed.

In the five levels of this literature series, you will be reading some of the greatest works of literature ever written. They are great not just because they are technically well done, though that certainly is a factor, but also because they reveal truth through the power of story.

EIL uses great literature, studied in its historic, literary, and artistic contexts, to help you learn to think and write analytically. This book is designed for students to use independently, so it contains specific instructions for each assignment, and a suggested schedule, as well as the references you need in order to do the background reading and research for each module.

You may be surprised to find I have not provided a lengthy introduction and a lot of background material for each book and author. This is because you have reached the age when you can assume responsibility for learning. Rather than spoon-feeding you basic, easily researched information (and having you zone out in the middle of paragraph two), I have provided resources and links that will enable you to perform the contextual research needed to fully understand the focus text. This is the kind of research you will be doing for college courses, so if you learn how to do it now, you should be quite good at it by the time you graduate!

How to Benefit from This Guide

To gain the greatest possible benefit from your literature study, you are responsible for reading this entire guide. Read the sections before and after the modules before you start working on the assignments. In the first section, you will find an explanation of how EIL works, suggestions for how to create a study routine and organize your study materials, chapters on how to read analytically and how to write essays. Following this you will find the syllabus section, with a study outline and schedule for each module. In the final section you will find instructions for writing specific types of papers, information for your writing mentor on how to evaluate papers, and sample papers that demonstrate correct MLA format (if you do not know what that is, be patient—it is explained in the samples and the glossary). Be sure to read all the chapters so you can be successful as you work through the assignments.

Each level of EIL has nine modules. Each module is intended to be completed in four relatively brief, but intense, weeks, though your writing mentor may decide to spend more or less time on a particular module. You may choose to group the modules into a traditional nine-month school year, or to use a four weeks on, one week off schedule. For a weekly routine, our family loosely followed a college-style block schedule in which we studied the humanities (literature, history, art, and music) in 2- to 3 hour blocks of time on Tuesday and Thursday; and math, science, and related subjects on Monday and Wednesday, but you are free to do what works best for you and your family.

Each assignment has been carefully chosen and scheduled so that knowledge and skills can build cumulatively, even if your writing mentor changes the order in which you study the modules. It is important that you learn time management skills that will help you complete assignments with minimal stress. If you are working with a writing mentor such as your parent, a writing evaluator, a coach, or a co-op instructor, be sure to agree in advance on a schedule, so that you can plan your work efficiently. Above all, do not spend three weeks procrastinating; then try to cram the assigned reading and writing into one week. Believe me, it does not work!

Course Format

Excellence in Literature courses are designed to focus in depth on selected great authors or literary movements, while exploring the context of the author's life and work through additional reading and writing. This offers opportunity to practice writing in a number of different formats, as well as the opportunity to grow thoroughly familiar with some of the greatest writers and literary works of all time.

Audio Books

Although many students are visual learners and do well reading each novel, auditory[1] or kinesthetic learners may benefit from listening to unabridged versions of the more challenging works. Epic poems such as *Beowulf* or *Paradise Lost* work especially well in audio, as it becomes easier to appreciate the rhythm and cadence of the language. The goal is for you to thoroughly understand and enjoy the material we cover, so use the learning tools that work best for you.

Context Materials

For each module there will be additional material to read, listen to, or watch. These resources are designed to provide contextual information that will help you understand the focus work. These context resources include links to interesting and informative websites, and recommendations for additional readings. Many of these are hosted or linked at Excellence-in-Literature.com. Here is the master index: https://excellence-in-literature.com/curriculum-user-content/e1-context-resources/

Do not feel limited by these resource suggestions. I encourage you to find and include other resources, such as videos, field trips, or other useful books. The more rich and varied the context materials, the more vivid and interesting the focus text will seem. If you find a book or author you particularly enjoy, take the time to read more of his or her writings or broaden your research. EIL is a solid foundation, and it is designed to be flexible, so you can shape it to reflect your own interests.

---

[1]An auditory learner is one who learns best by hearing; a kinesthetic learner learns by doing.

Study Clusters

You may want to consider planning the high school years in study clusters—grouping American history with American literature, British history with British literature, and so forth. This reinforces learning and increases memorable context for both literature and history. You may mix and match EIL modules to fit the history you are studying.

The Honors Track

In each module, you will find additional reading suggestions under the "Honors" heading. If you would like to earn an honors-level grade (weighted by .5 grade point), you need to read an extra book and do an approach paper for each module. At the end of the school year, you will also write an additional research paper, which is assigned in the Honors chapter. This will complete the honors track.

To earn advanced placement or college credit for the class (weighted by 1.0 grade point), you will also need to take an AP or CLEP exam. You can find complete details on how to assign weighted grades and record advanced classes in my book, *Transcripts Made Easy* (www.TranscriptsMadeEasy.com). Additional information about how and why to earn college credits can be found in *Get a Jump Start on College!* (www.GetAJumpStartOnCollege.com).

Prerequisites for Success

Excellence in Literature is intended for use by students in grades 8–12. For each level, you are expected to have age-appropriate skills in grammar, spelling, and language mechanics. Students should grammar- and spell-check all papers before turning them in, as learning to self-edit is part of the writing process.

If you have not done literary analysis or essay writing, there are two resources I recommend. *Teaching the Classics* by Adam and Missy Andrews is a brief DVD course that teaches literary analysis using short works to illustrate the principles and methods. For essay writing, *The Elegant Essay Writing Lessons* by Lesha Myers is the best resource I have seen. Both are published by the Institute for Excellence in Writing, and both can be used concurrently with *Excellence in Literature*.

Is it better to own or to borrow books?

I have discovered that if you have books in your home, they will be read. I do not expect you to purchase all the resources I have referenced, but I hope you will consider having a few of the most important on hand. You can find them used at online retailers such as Amazon.com or Alibris.com, or you may even be able to get them free through PaperbackSwap.com (you may use my referral, "readbx"). I have purchased many books quite cheaply from library sales, thrift shops, and yard sales. Studies have shown that the number of books owned in a family has a direct relationship to the student's long-term academic success, with measurably higher test scores for book owners than for age mates with fewer books in the home.

For the focus texts, I encourage you to consider purchasing nice, annotated paperback editions because those books will become part of your student's mental furniture and may be read and reread many times. For most of the books, my favorite editions are Ignatius Critical Editions or Modern Library Press Paperback Classics. You can find links to most of the recommended texts at Excellence-in-Literature. com.

Learning Philosophy

Learn (lûrn) v. 1 Acquire knowledge of (a subject) or skill in (an art, etc.) as a result of study, experience, or instruction; acquire or develop an ability to do. 1.1 Commit to memory.

—Oxford Shorter English Dictionary

The foundation of the *Excellence in Literature* philosophy is the verb "learn." I believe the acquisition of knowledge and skills is an active endeavor. The process of learning is focused within one person—the learner. Just as an infant makes the transition from being fed to feeding himself, a student who wants to be successful will begin to take an active role in absorbing and understanding information that will help him interpret his world. Although many students wait until college to make this transition, high school is actually an ideal time to learn how to learn.

As a writer, my goal is to impart not only knowledge, but also the tools and skills you need to take an active part in the learning process. I have always been a reader and an active learner, and I know from experience that the process is fascinating and invigorating. If you are an active learner, you will rarely be bored, and you can be confident in your ability to learn and do almost anything. There is great joy in learning, and this, above all, is what I want to communicate.

The Learning Process: Roles of Excellence in Literature, the Student, and the Writing Mentor

The EIL guide will

- Establish the scope and sequence for the class.
- Assign appropriate readings.
- Provide a suggested schedule for assignments.
- Provide time management and organization tips.
- Provide a rubric for objectively evaluating completed assignments.

The Student will

- Study this book and understand the sequence and timing of assignments.
- Ask questions of the writing mentor when something is not clearly understood.
- Actively seek to learn from each assignment.
- Complete all assignments on time.
- Make no excuses.
- Enjoy great literature.

The Writing Mentor (teacher or parent) will

- Help the student obtain required books and reference materials.
- Verify that assignments are completed on schedule.
- Use the rubric or select a qualified writing evaluator to provide feedback for the student.
- Provide an evaluation summary for the year, using the form found at the end of this book.

*Note: Week 3 assignments and those marked with an asterisk have instructions and a model for imitation. See Formats and Models chapter for details.
Module "Introduction" includes "Something to think about . . ." and "Be sure to notice . . ." paragraphs.

Excellence in Literature Pacing Chart

Suggested pacing of modules: Move through nine modules per school year, adapting your pace as needed.

WEEK	What to Read	What to Write	Module Focus	Optional Honors Reading	Optional Honors Writing
1	Read book introductory material; Module 1.1 Introduction, A White Heron and Context Resources	Read A White Heron	Learn to write an approach paper; consider the five elements of fiction, Plot, Theme, Characterization, Setting, and Style; write a basic compare/contrast essay.		
2	Read remaining short stories	Literature Summary* for each short story		At least one additional short story from each author; biographical information	
3					
4		Write a first draft and turn in for feedback; edit/revise assignment; turn in.			Approach Paper*
5	Module 1.2 Introduction, Around the World in Eighty Days and Context Resources	Author Profile*	Victorian focus on travel, exoticism, and the "shrinking world"		
6		Approach Paper*			
7		Write a first draft and turn in for feedback.		20,000 Leagues Under the Sea	
8		Edit and revise assignment; turn in.			Approach Paper*
9	Module 1.3 Introduction, A Connecticut Yankee in King Arthur's Court, and Context Resources	Author Profile*	Use of irony and framed narrative to address serious issues		
10		Approach Paper* or graphic storyline			
11		Write a first draft and turn in for feedback.		The Prince and the Pauper	
12		Edit and revise essay; turn in.			Approach Paper*
13	Module 1.4 Introduction, Jane Eyre and Context Resources	Author Profile*	Medieval worldview		
14		Three journal entries in the voice of Jane Eyre			
15		Write a first draft and turn in for feedback.		Villette and/or Shirley	
16		Edit and revise essay; turn in.			Approach Paper*

*Note: Assignments marked with an asterisk have a model for imitation. See Formats and Models chapter for details..

Excellence in Literature Pacing Chart

Suggested Pacing of Modules: Move through nine modules each school year, adapting your pace as needed.

WEEK	What to Read	What to Write	Module Focus	Optional Honors Reading	Optional Honors Writing
17		Rewrite the legend in a modern setting			
18	Module 1.5 Introduction, Bullfinch legend, *Pygmalion*, and Context Resources	Author Profile*	Continuity of plot in a variety of literary forms		
19		Write a first draft and turn in for feedback.			
20		Edit and revise assignment; turn in.		*Murder in the Cathedral*	Approach Paper*
21	Module 1.6 Introduction, *Treasure Island*, and Context Resources	Author Profile*			
22		Historical Period/Event Approach Paper* on the Golden Age of Piracy	Characteristics of classic quest tale		
23		Write a first draft and turn in for feedback.		*Kidnapped*	
24		Edit and revise essay; turn in.			Approach Paper*
25	Module 1.7 Introduction, Context Resources, and *Animal Farm*	Author Profile*			
26		Character list; Historical Period/Event Approach Paper* on the Russian Revolution	Political satire in the form of a beast fable		
27		Write a first draft and turn in for feedback.		*1984* and *Fahrenheit 451*	
28		Edit and revise assignment; turn in.			Approach Paper*
29	Module 1.8 Introduction, *The Tempest*, and Context Resources	Author Profile*			
30		Scene Summaries	Literary concepts of romance and comedy; Shakespeare's characterizations		
31		Write a first draft and turn in for feedback.		*A Midsummer Night's Dream*	
32		Edit and revise assignment; turn in.			Approach Paper*

	Author Profile*		The Pilgrim's Progress	Approach Paper*
33	Module 1.9 Introduction, *Gulliver's Travels*, and Context Resources			
34	Historical Period/Event Approach Paper* on the European Enlightenment (Age of Reason)	The use of satire to attack the ideas of the Enlightenment	*The Pilgrim's Progress*	
35	Write a first draft and turn in for feedback.			
36	Edit and revise assignment; turn in.			

Index of context resource links: https://excellence-in-literature.com/curriculum-user-content/e1-context-resources/.

Getting Started

Before you begin, set up a study area and English notebook to help you stay organized. If you learn how to do this now, you will be a step ahead when you get to college and realize that you are completely responsible for creating a time and place to learn. College professors usually hand out a syllabus at the first class, with all the assignments and due dates for the semester. They do not remind you of what is coming up, so if you do not have a method for keeping on top of everything, you can quickly fall behind. You will find the organizational techniques you learn from EIL helpful for any class you take in the future.

What belongs in a study area?

Study area basics are a comfortable chair, bright light, your English notebook and reading log, calendar or datebook, good dictionary, thesaurus, writer's handbook, pens, pencils, paper, sticky notes such as Post-it® notes, and possibly a computer. Being organized will make your study time more pleasant and productive, so be sure to start the school year by pulling together these things.

How to Use Items in Your Study Area

Chair and light: Read here (see the chapter on "How to Read a Book"). You want to be comfortable enough to enjoy the experience, but not so comfortable that you fall asleep. It is pleasant to read near a window, but you should also have a reading light positioned so that the light falls on your book. If you find that your eyes get tired quickly, you may need a brighter light or even reading glasses. Do not hesitate to get your eyes checked, so you can enjoy reading.

Calendar: Use a calendar or planner to record assignment deadlines, field trips, and other activities. At the beginning of each module, check the number of pages in your focus text and number of context resources; then plan how many you need to read daily in order to finish the focus text before you begin the essay.

English notebook: Organize your English papers in a three-ring binder. You can use page protectors that hold two sheets back-to-back, or you can punch holes and put everything directly into the binder. The first thing you should see when you open the cover is a list of modules and assignments (look for the form right after the evaluation summary). Next, put in a copy of each assignment you do, along with your note pages and the evaluation rubrics you receive. You may want to have a glossary section at the end with lists of new words you have learned, so you can review them easily.

Reading log: List everything you read—not just the books you read for English, but everything. Write the title, author, a one- or two-sentence summary of the book, and a comment or rating. A blank journal is handy for this, or you may prefer to keep the record in a database on your computer. There is even a form in my book, *Transcripts Made Easy*, that you can reproduce and use.

Dictionary: Look up unfamiliar words you encounter. If you can guess their meaning from the context, just write down the word on a small sticky note and stick it on the page. Look it up after you are finished reading. If you cannot guess the meaning from the context, look it up before continuing. Looking up challenging words not only builds vocabulary and helps you remember the word, but also reveals the nuances in meaning that set the word apart from its synonyms. My favorite dictionary is the *Oxford Shorter English Dictionary* because most of the word usage examples are from literature, but most college dictionaries are acceptable as well.

Thesaurus: Use this when you find yourself repeating the same descriptive words over and over. I use *Roget A to Z*, which is organized alphabetically. The English language is fascinating, and there is a perfect word for almost any occasion—please find it and use it!

EIL Handbook for Writers, Writers Inc., or other handbook: Cannot remember when to use a comma or a semicolon? Here is where you go to find out. Need instructions for how to write an expository essay? You will find it in your writer's handbook. A professional writer or editor always has several frequently used handbooks nearby. Writer's handbooks are packed with great information, and the reason professionals have several is that different handbooks have different areas of focus. No matter how competent you are as a writer, there is no way you can remember every tiny detail of grammar, style, or usage, so it pays to check your handbook—chances are, you will find exactly the help you need.

Pens: Use a pen for mind mapping (thinking on paper) rough drafts, illustrations, Venn diagrams, and more. When I was in college, one of my favorite ways to study a long, challenging work was to use an 18" x 24" sketch pad and multi colored gel pens. I spent one semester in an in-depth independent study of Edmund Spenser's *The Fairie Queene* and found that the best way to see themes and remember what happened where was to summarize each book of the poem with a quick sketch (stick figures) and bullet points illustrating each canto.

Pencils: These are for writing in your books. Yes, I mean it—I want you to underline key passages, talk back to the characters, note thoughts that occur to you as you read, and so forth. This is called annotation, and it is part of active reading (you will learn more about this in the "How to Read a Book" chapter). Taking notes in the text will help you get the most out of a story. If you have to use library books for your focus texts, you will not be able to annotate as easily, but you can put a piece of paper in the back of the book and use it for the things you would normally write in the book.

Sticky notes: One of the first things to do is to make sticky-note tabs for your writer's handbook. This helps you turn quickly to key pages. For classes using an anthology, I recommend that at the beginning of the semester you look at the syllabus and go through the anthology and place a sticky-note tab with the author's last name and the title of the work beside each assigned piece. This saves time and helps remind you of what you have covered, and what remains.

Computer: When you reach college or the business world, you will need to know how to use a computer, so high school is the time to become comfortable with its basic functions. Rather than using a word-processing program on your computer, I suggest learning to use the free online word-processing program by Google. It is accessible through any Internet-connected computer, and your paper can be easily shared with a writing instructor, no matter where he or she is located.

Computer Tips

Formatting papers: Once you are in high school, all written work should be submitted in a college-style format. This means it should be typed in Times New Roman or a similar font, double-spaced, with one-inch margins all around (see the sample paper in the back of this book). Be sure to have the grammar- and spell-check turned on in your word processing program, but do not rely too heavily on these checking tools, because they are often wrong. Always do a "human proofread" by reading your paper aloud to yourself before turning it in. Reading aloud helps you slow down enough to spot typos and hear sentences or phrases that do not flow smoothly.

One space after terminal punctuation: Space only once after any terminal punctuation (period, question mark, etc.). Old typing instruction books used to require two spaces after terminal punctuation because typewriters use what is called a mono-spaced type, and the double spacing helped the eye distinguish the end of a sentence. Computer fonts are proportionally spaced, and proper spacing is programmed in. Double spacing creates unattractive blobs of white down a page and is a dead giveaway that outdated methods are being used.

Saving your document: Always create a computer folder for each class, and use a descriptive file name when you save your papers. For example, if you are writing the essay on Benjamin Franklin's *Autobiography* from the first module of American Literature, name the file "eil3-u1-franklin," and it will be easy to find anytime you need it.

If a paper gets "lost" on your computer: If you are new to the world of computers, you may occasionally think you have lost something on your computer. If you have been typing and your text seems to disappear, try pressing the Command key along with Z. This is the "undo" command, and it will undo the last thing you did, which should bring your paper back into view. If it does not, you can search your hard drive for the file name you used when you saved it. If you are using a Mac computer or Google Docs, any document should easily be found.

Frequently Asked Questions

Be curious always! For knowledge will not acquire you; you must acquire it.

—Sudie Back

If you have questions about any aspect of the curriculum or about studying in general, you may find the answers in this chapter.

Are all assignment instructions contained in this book?

This EIL guide contains the outline of the course, an assignment schedule for each module, models of the type of papers you will be writing, and evaluation information. In addition, you will need a copy of each of the novel-length focus works and a writer's handbook.

It is helpful to have old editions of Norton Anthologies of American, British, and World Literature for additional information and readings for each historical period. Beyond the basics, an atlas, art history book, and a dictionary of allusions are excellent optional additions to the study and reference tools listed here and in the "Getting Started" chapter.

You do not tell me how many pages to read each day. How will I know?

It is all about time management! This is a college-prep class, so you will be learning to look ahead and pace yourself. For modules based upon a novel-length work, you have a couple of options: 1) Sit down the first day and read the whole book in several hours; then use the rest of the time to gather supporting information; perhaps read another book by the author; and write your essay; or 2) Divide the book into two equal parts, and read one part per week, leaving the last two weeks to write and polish your essay. I prefer the first method, as the story is usually more interesting if it is not read in tiny fragments over a long period of time. This also leaves plenty of time to draft, revise, and polish your essay.

C. S. Lewis wrote that "a narrative style is not to be judged by snippets. You must read for at least half a day and read with your mind on the story" (from *English Literature in the Sixteenth Century Excluding Drama*). He is a wise guide, because immersion changes the experience of reading from an assignment to a journey into another world, another place, and another time. Whatever you do, start reading the first day of the module, and read every day until the book is finished. Do not procrastinate. And do not forget your context readings!

Can I use library books, or do I have to buy them?

I encourage active reading that includes annotation, especially of the focus works. This means underlining and making notes in the margin, and librarians really hate that. So I recommend you buy the focus books. You can probably find used copies fairly cheaply.

Do you recommend a particular edition of each book?

It is important to have books that are pleasant to hold and read so that you enjoy the process and do not suffer from eyestrain. I do not recommend mass-market paperbacks, since they usually have too-small type, very small margins, and no scholarly introduction or discussion questions. Many are so hard to hold open that the spine is soon broken.

My favorite editions include Ignatius Critical Editions (best notes), Modern Library Paperback Classics. Norton, Penguin, and Oxford. The newest editions from these publishers are designed to lie open like a hardback, and they usually have insightful introductions and good discussion questions at the end. You will find links to each of my recommended editions at ExcellenceinLiterature.com.

Can I read the focus texts on an e-reader?

You can read the texts on an e-reader such as the Kindle® or Nook®, but it is not always easy to annotate as you are reading or to page back to look up a character or event. In addition, if you use free versions from the public domain, be aware that the available translations may not be of the best quality. If you decide to use an e-reader, be sure to learn how to highlight and add notes and bookmarks.

The assignment said to write a 500-word essay. I accidentally wrote 603 words. What shall I do?

You can edit to make your work tighter, which will usually make your paper better. As Strunk and White admonish in *Elements of Style*, it is best to "omit needless words." The second option is to not worry about it. The word count is a minimum rather than a maximum requirement. It is stated as number of words rather than number of pages so that teachers will not receive essays with 16-point type and 2" margins, because someone had to fill three pages and had no ideas. Word count allows no fudging.

What should go into the assignment header?

Every paper you turn in should have a proper heading as shown in the sample papers in the Formats and Models chapter. The heading should include your first and last name, the class name with the instructor's name on the same line, the date, and the essay prompt. The essay prompt is included to make it easy for the evaluator to determine whether your essay is on topic, and it is especially important for modules in which you have a choice of topics.

How do I download and print items from the Internet?

If you have done some Internet research, or if I have provided a link or URL to a resource you need to download and print, you can follow these steps:

1. Copy (control + c) the entire underlined URL, and paste (control + v) it into the address window of your browser, and click "enter."

2. If the page that appears offers a link to a printable copy, click the link to print directly from the screen.

3. If there is no link to a printable copy, hold down the left button of your mouse, and drag to select the text you want to copy.

4. Copy and paste the text into a blank TextEdit or Notepad file, and save it to your English folder or to a Google Drive or Evernote.com account online.

5. Go back to the web page where you found the information. Select the URL in the address line, and copy and paste it at the end of your text. Type in the date you accessed the website and any other information you think may be important. You may need some of this information for your Works Cited page. Remember that it is never okay to copy material from anywhere and turn it in as your own work.

Why are there a lot of Internet resources?

First, they are free and globally available. If you do not have a computer with Internet access, chances are that you can use one at your local library or at a friend's house. Second, you need to know how to use a computer responsibly, and how to find the kind of resources you will need for the future, whether that future involves college, business, or teaching your own children. My goal is to introduce you to a lot of useful sites and resources, and to make you aware of what is available. As an ongoing project, we have begun to host many of these resources at our own Excellence-in-Literature.com website, so they will always be easily available. You will find the most updated list of links for this level at:

https://excellence-in-literature.com/curriculum-user-content/e1-context-resources/

What happens if a link does not work?

The context resource links on Excellence-in-Literature.com are regularly updated, but if you have a problem with a link not loading, just type a few words of the title or author's name in the search box at Excellence-in-Literature.com, and the resource should show up if it is hosted there.

If you do not see the resource on EIL, double-check each character you have typed, and make sure it matches the link provided. If you are using an e-book and you copy and paste the link, be sure not to pick up any punctuation near the link because that will keep it from working.

Finally, if you are sure you have typed the link correctly, and you are not getting to the page, try doing a Google search for some of the keywords in the resource. For example, if the link for the Mark Twain House and Museum does not work, type "mark twain house museum" into your browser's search box, and the correct resource should come up in the results.

Do I have to read everything?

There are two things you absolutely must read, and they are this entire guide and each of the focus texts. I would like for you to read most of the context materials, but in a few cases there are more than you need. I have often included more than one suggested biography, simply because there are several good ones to choose from, and you may pick whichever one is easily available. The goal is for you to learn what you need to know in order to understand the author and the text and to write a thoughtful essay, not to just check off a random bunch of stuff.

I thought this was English class. Why do I have to look at art and listen to music?

Literature is a unique representation of its culture. Each great work was written by an author who was influenced by books, people, art, music, and events of his day. These influences, coupled with the author's education and family life, shaped the worldview that is inevitably reflected in his work.

In order to understand a poem, play, or story, it helps to understand a bit about the author and his or her philosophy of life. The biographical sketches can help with this, but sampling the art and music the author could have seen or heard is a different and sometimes more compelling way of gaining insight. The sights and sounds of an era can also help to illuminate the philosophy of life that shaped the focus text. You can think of content exploration as a virtual field trip!

How much time will EIL take each day?

The amount of time you spend depends on the length of the focus text and your reading speed. As an average, plan to spend at least one hour per day reading or writing about the focus text. Separate context reading or vocabulary work may add an additional 20–45 minutes per day.

Our family is different—do we have to follow the schedule exactly as it is written?

The schedule I have provided is the one my students followed when I taught these courses online (which I no longer do). It works efficiently and will help you enjoy all the books over the course of the school year. In addition, I arranged the modules to provide variation in type of reading and writing, and the modules graduate in difficulty from the beginning to the end of the year. However, I completely understand that each situation is unique. You may change the schedule, drop a module, take two years to cover the book, or alter it in any way that will help it better serve your family.

If you are teaching EIL in a co-op or school, you have the same liberty, though students who are following along in the book can probably be counted on to remind you that "That's not what Mrs. Campbell said to do!" Whatever you do, I promise that the EIL Enforcement Department will *not* stop by to rap your knuckles. The curriculum is here to serve you, and I want you to enjoy using it.

Why read old books?

There are many reasons to read old books, but author and apologist C. S. Lewis simply suggests that it is necessary in order to "keep the clean sea breeze of the centuries blowing through our minds" and to escape the "characteristic blindness of the twentieth century." He writes:

> It is a good rule, after reading a new book, never to allow yourself another new one till you have read an old one in between. If that is too much for you, you should at least read one old one to every three new ones.
>
> Every age has its own outlook. It is specially good at seeing certain truths and specially liable to make certain mistakes. We all, therefore, need the books that will correct the characteristic mistakes of our own period. And that means the old books. All contemporary writers share to some extent the contemporary outlook—even those, like myself, who seem most opposed to it . . . The only palliative is to keep the clean sea breeze of the centuries blowing through our minds, and this can be done only by reading old books . . . Two heads are better than one, not because either is infallible, but because they are unlikely to go wrong in the same direction. (From an introduction by C. S. Lewis to a translation of *Athanasius: On the Incarnation*. Read the entire essay online at http://www.spurgeon. org/~phil/history/ath-inc.htm.)

In another good essay on this topic, Professor Dominic Manganiello, D.Phil., explains to his students, "We will read old books, then, because in the past lie the foundations of our present and future hope. We will discover that the writings of the masters deal with 'primal and conventional things . . . the hunger for bread, the love of woman, the love of children, the desire for immortal life.'" The remainder of this essay can be found at http://www.augustinecollege.org/papers/DM_7Sept98.htm.

Finally, in perhaps the most compelling reason of all, Alexandr Solzhenitsyn pointed out that "literature conveys irrefutable condensed experience in yet another invaluable direction; namely, from generation to generation. Thus it becomes the living memory of the nation. Thus it preserves and kindles within itself the flame of her spent history, in a form which is safe from deformation and slander. In this way literature, together with language, protects the soul of the nation." You may read his entire 1970 Nobel Lecture at http://www.nobelprize.org/nobel_prizes/literature/ laureates/1970/solzhenitsyn-lecture.html.

How to Read a Book

Some books are meant to be tasted, some swallowed, and some few digested . . .

—Francis Bacon

No, you have not picked up the wrong course by mistake—this is indeed high school English! I know you have been reading for years, but I want you to learn to read actively and analytically. I will review the basics of reading fiction and poetry here, so that you will have an idea of how to read and analyze throughout each of the Excellence in Literature courses.

If you are using any level of EIL and you have not thoroughly studied literary analysis, I recommend going through Adam Andrews' excellent *Teaching the Classics* DVD course. This 8-hour course teaches the structure and elements of literature and Socratic discussion using short stories. This course is brief enough that it can be used over the summer before you begin EIL, or even concurrently. *A CiRCE Guide to Reading* is an excellent short reference book that is an excellent companion to *Teaching the Classics.*

If you are studying English III, IV, or V, you may also want to read *How to Read a Book,* Mortimer Adler and Charles Van Doren's comprehensive, classic guide to the art of reading,. For other perspectives on literary analysis, you may find the resources by James W. Sire and Gene Edward Veith (listed in the resources section at the end of this guide) helpful. Each of these resources can help you become a better reader and thinker.

Reading great literature is about much more than just skimming over the words on a page. It is a process that involves absorbing, understanding, and making decisions about what the author is communicating. Reading is active and can be as richly rewarding as you want it to be. Quick, fun reading can help you practice basic reading skills, but you will need to add analysis in order to grow as a reader and writer. I hope you will enjoy the learning process.

Reading Challenging Literature

The classics tell some of the most interesting, thought-provoking stories of all time. That is one reason that they have become classic. Because writers of earlier centuries lived and wrote a bit differently from modern storytellers, their works can seem challenging, or even a bit dull if you do not fully understand them. Here are some of ways you will gain understanding in the Excellence in Literature modules.

- The key to enjoying any great book is to approach it first as a story. Read or listen all the way through, just as you would if you were reading *The Lord of the Rings* or any other book you enjoy.

- Read all the way through, at a comfortable pace. Read fast enough to sustain interest, but slowly enough to understand what is happening.

- Read brief contextual information about the author and the historical time in which the book, poem, or play was written.

- For the most challenging books, you may begin by reading a children's version or a brief synopsis of the work. This is not necessary for most works, but I have assigned it for those with archaic language, such as Chaucer's *Canterbury Tales* or for epic poetry such as Homer's *Odyssey*. Once you have read the synopsis or children's version of a difficult book, you will be ready to read or listen to the complete text.

- If the assignment is poetry or a play, listen to it (even if you have to read it aloud to yourself in order to do so) or watch it as suggested in the assignments. Poetry is meant to be heard, and plays are meant to be seen and heard, so you must do this in order to fully appreciate them.

- Use the context resources to get acquainted with the art, music, poetry, and other literature relevant to the author or focus text. This helps you understand the author's artistic and cultural influences and can give you insight as to why the author wrote the story he/she wrote in the way that it is written.

- As you read, keep an index card or piece of paper tucked into the back of the book, or write on the blank end pages. When you encounter words you do not know, do not interrupt the flow of the story as long as you understand the basic meaning from the context—just write down the word and look it up later.

- In your English notebook write down interesting insights that occur to you, as well as quotes that seem significant. Feel free to mark important or interesting passages in the book (see the "Annotating" section later in this chapter) so that you can easily find them again while writing your essay.

- Once you have read the book, start the writing assignments. If you are working with a book not listed in this guide, write an approach paper according to the instructions in the Formats and Models chapter. The approach paper should include a brief summary, character analysis, discussion questions, key passage, and an explanation of the key passage. This will help you think through the book and prepare you for writing an essay.

- Write the assigned essay in response to the essay prompt. Believe it or not, writing thoughtfully about something specific in the book helps you gain insights you wouldn't otherwise have. Writing helps you learn!

Reading Fiction

If you are reading fiction, you will need to notice how the five elements of **plot, theme, character, setting, and style** work together to create the alternate world of the story. However, while you are reading, it is also important to allow yourself to be immersed in the fictional world, to the point that when you stop reading, you feel as if you have just returned from a long journey. Immersion allows you to experience the author's creation as he or she intended. It also helps you to see the story as a whole when you begin to analyze the elements of the text.

As you read, try to not only understand the surface meaning of the text, but also underlying themes. Thinking about or discussing the list of questions at the end of this chapter can help you move deeper into the text and prepare for the writing assignments.

As you look through the questions, you may find literary terms you do not know. Look them up in the Glossary of this guide, and if you need more information, consult your writer's handbook, or go to Google and type in "define:" (without the quotes) followed by the word or phrase you are looking for.

Reading Poetry

If you are reading poetry, there are a few other things to consider. Poetry uses structure, sound, and syntax to awaken the reader's imagination and to convey an image or message in a vivid and memorable way. A beautifully written poem can convey an idea in just a few unforgettable lines. If you have not studied the analysis of poetry, it is especially important to review the process in one or more of the resources I have recommended above, such as *How to Read a Book* or your writer's handbook.

To begin understanding a poem, read it through slowly and carefully at least once or twice. Read it aloud, and listen to the sound of the words and pacing of the lines and syllables. Once you have the sound of the poem in your head, try paraphrasing it in prose. Think about each element and how the structure of the lines and the sound of the words contributes to the poem's theme. Examine the images, the rhyme scheme, and the sound patterns of the poem to help you understand the poet's message. Above all, read it through (or listen to it) in its entirety often enough that you see and remember it as a whole, just as you would look at a great painting as a whole before beginning to study the brush strokes.

Comedy and Tragedy

Although we sometimes think of comedy as something funny and tragedy as something sad, these words have a slightly different meaning in the study of literature. Comedy is a story that begins with a conflict or suffering and ends in joy, such as *Jane Eyre* or *A Midsummer Night's Dream*.

Tragedy is a story that begins at a high point and ends in pain, such as *Romeo and Juliet* or *Oedipus Rex*. In Veith's interesting chapter on comedy and tragedy, he suggests that the upward movement in comedy reflects a redemptive storyline, while the downward movement of tragedy reflects the archetypal fall of humanity. Aristotle further defined tragedy as the downfall of a noble human, in a disaster of his own making (*King Lear*).

Facing Challenging Ideas

Great literature tends to mirror life. A book becomes a classic because it creates an honest and true picture of life and accurately depicts the consequences of various philosophies of life. In portraying life accurately, complex and sometimes unpleasant issues arise, just as they do in life. Characters do or say things that are deeply wrong, as Macbeth did in giving way to ambition and committing murder, or Peter Rabbit did in stealing carrots from Mr. MacGregor's garden. However, each character experienced appropriate, true-to-life consequences for his actions, which makes it possible for the reader to identify with and learn from the story.

Gene Edward Veith specifically cautions Christian readers not to "seize upon a detail [such as a "bad word"] or a subject dealt with by a book, take it completely out of context, and fail to do the necessary labor of thinking about the work and interpreting it thematically" (72) before taking a stand against the book. He also cautions against stories that do not tell the truth about life. "Stories filled with 'good people' overcoming all odds may create the dangerous impression that human beings are, in fact, 'good' and capable of saving themselves through their own moral actions" (76). This type of plot is often found in genre fiction—what I call "Twinkies® for the brain"—and is what keeps these books from being great literature even when they tell an enjoyable story.

Annotating

If you annotate your books as you read, you will understand and enjoy them more deeply than if you simply skim the text. Your annotations will also help you quickly locate important scenes in the book as you are doing the writing assignments for each module. Here are some suggestions for effective annotation.

Use a pencil for all writing in your books, as it does not show through and can be erased if necessary. Write on the inside of the covers or on the blank pages at the front and back of your focus text. Use an index card or piece of paper if you are using a library book.

- **Draw a vertical line** or star beside significant paragraphs you would like to remember.
- **Underline** important phrases or ideas.
- **Character List:** List each of the characters in the order in which they appear. Include a brief note about the character's role in the plot or any distinguishing characteristics. I do this inside the front cover.
- **Timeline:** List each major event in the story as it happens. The inside back cover is a good place for this.
- **Context:** If the focus text mentions a person, a piece of art, literature, or music, or a historic event, make a note in the margin and look up the item. Many classical compositions can be found on YouTube.com. Just search by typing in the composer or composition name.
- **Questions:** If you have a question about something in the text, write it in the margin. Writing it down will help you recognize the answer if it later appears in the text. If it does not appear, the written question will remind you to do a bit more research.

Questions to Consider as You Read

If you are not familiar with the terms used in this list, look them up in the Glossary at the back of the guide or in your writer's handbook. These questions may help you think through some of the stories or may be useful in a discussion, but you do not need to spend a lot of time with them.

- Should [character name] do [whatever he/she is planning]? Why or why not? (This is the most interesting question for discussion!)

- What happens, and in what order does it happen (plot)?

- What does it mean? What great ideas (justice, friendship, good vs. evil, etc.) are being illustrated in the story (theme)?

- What can you learn, or what do you think the author believes you should do or not do?

- Who is the **narrator** of the story, and is he or she reliable?

- How do the characters embody the theme of the story?

- Who are the major and minor characters, and what kind of people are they? Consider physical, mental, moral, and spiritual dimensions.

- Do the challenges of the main character reflect common struggles of humanity? Is the character intended to portray an archetype?

- Can you identify the basic stages of the story structure—exposition (background information), rising action (complications), climax, falling action, resolution?

- How is the story told? Possibilities include first-person narrative, a journal, epistolary style (told as a series of letters), etc. How does this method affect your understanding of each of the story elements?

- Does the method of storytelling affect your enjoyment of the plot?

- What **symbolism** do you see, and how effectively does it enhance your understanding?

- What types of **conflict** do you see? Possibilities include man vs. man, man vs. God, man vs. nature, man vs. society, or even man vs. himself.

- What role does each character play in revealing the story?

- What **plot devices** does the author use to move the story along? Possibilities include flashbacks, narrative frames, foreshadowing, genre-specific conventions, and so forth.

- Why has the author used a specific word rather than a synonym in the way and in the place he has used it? Would a synonym work as well? Why or why not?

How to Write an Essay

The time to begin writing an article is when you have finished it to your satisfaction. By that time you begin to clearly and logically perceive what it is you really want to say.

—Mark Twain

An essay is a short writing assignment on a particular subject. According to the *Oxford Shorter English Dictionary*, the word *essay* is derived from the Latin root *exigere*, which means to ascertain or weigh. It is also defined as "a first tentative attempt at learning, composition, etc.; a first draft." The essay is sometimes called a position paper, because it must be an expression of the writer's judgment, rather than a simple report.

Essays can be written to inform an audience, explain something, argue a position, or analyze an issue. Because the writer is expressing an opinion or interpretation, each essay can be seen as an attempt to persuade the reader that your thesis is plausible. Because the essay form involves all steps of the writing process, you will be able to apply the skills learned to any type of writing you do in the future.

In Excellence in Literature, you will have the opportunity to write essays, approach papers, literature summaries, and author profiles. The essay prompt in each module will provide an exact subject, and you will find that writing itself will turn into a process of discovery. You will rarely know the answer to the questions in the essay prompt until you begin writing, but as you begin to formulate a thesis and write analytically, you will begin to understand the subject at a much deeper level than if you had simply read the book.

The Writing Process

The three canons of classical composition are Invention, Arrangement, and Elocution.

- Invention, also called Discovery, is the process of coming up with ideas;
- Arrangement, otherwise known as Disposition, is the process of placing ideas in logical order;
- Elocution, sometimes referred to as Style, is the process of appropriately expressing ideas.

Essentially, every writer must gather ideas, put them in order, and write them in a way that is understandable and appealing. To do this, I recommend the following writing process:

1. Invention
   - Read/Research
   - Think on Paper
2. Arrangement
   - Organize Ideas
3. Elocution
   - Write
   - Revise

Read and Research

To begin an essay assignment, gather information through reading and research. For Excellence in Literature assignments, this means you will read the focus text and assigned context resources, plus any other resources that seem relevant. Be sure to choose research materials from reliable sources such as published encyclopedias and reference books, college websites, and original source documents.

Think on Paper with a Mind Map

To Think on Paper, the second step of the writing process, you will begin to connect reading and research with the essay prompt. I use the process of mind mapping as a tool for thinking on paper. This allows ideas and supporting points to be quickly recorded in an organic form that encourages the flow of ideas. Here is an example of a simple mind map.

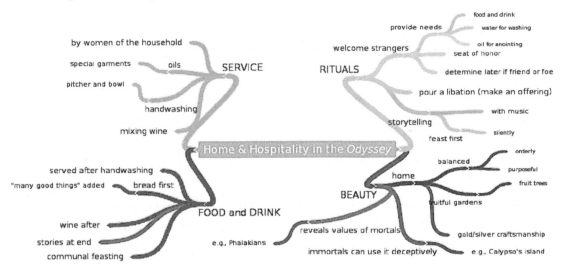

How to Think on Paper

- At the center of your paper, write a few words that summarize the topic or question you are supposed to answer.

- Draw a line radiating from the center idea for each relevant fact, possible argument, proof point, or supporting detail that comes to mind.

- Branch off these ideas as additional details emerge.

- Write down everything that comes to mind, even if you are not sure it fits. Generating ideas is like turning on a faucet for hot water. What comes out at first is not hot, but it has to come out before what you really want can emerge. Your best ideas usually begin to flow after your mind has warmed up and settled into thinking about a topic.

- Record each idea on the mind map as a word or phrase rather than a complete sentence, and feel free to use symbols and abbreviations to briefly capture your idea.

Additional Mind Mapping Ideas

- You may use color in your mind maps, but it is best not to create an elaborate color coding scheme, as this can impede the flow of ideas.

- Some people prefer to use quick sketches rather than words to capture some or all of their ideas. If this is the way your mind works, and it does not slow you down too much, you may do this.

- Mind maps are usually made with pen or pencil on paper, but the sample above was created with a free web app called Coggle.it. Do what works for you.

- You can see many examples of mind maps at http://www.tonybuzan.com/gallery/mind-maps/

Organize Ideas

Once you have generated several ideas, you must decide which ideas best fit the essay assignment, and how they might logically flow. Begin by dividing ideas into three categories: Affirmative, Negative, and Interesting (sometimes known as Pro, Con, and Interesting). Once you have categorized ideas, you will probably have more than you need, so select the most compelling points, and either number them on your mind map, or list them in a logical sequence.

Look at the ordered ideas, and determine whether your thesis will be an Affirmative or Negative answer to the essay prompt, or whether you will take an equivocal position in which you provide evidence for and against both sides of the question.

Thesis Statement

Draft a thesis statement that outlines your position and describes how you will support your argument. In its most elementary form, the thesis can be as simple as a transformation of the essay prompt into a thesis statement. Here is an example of what this looks like:

Question (adapted from a portion of the essay prompt in *American Literature* Module 2):

- How did the courtship strategies of Irving's characters compare to those of Longfellow's characters?

Question transformed into a thesis statement:

- Although Bram Bones and John Alden were successful in their respective courtships, their courtship strategies differed from one another in several specific ways, including [insert three ways here].

The thesis statement would usually appear near the end of the introductory paragraph, completing the job of orienting the reader to the topic and your position.

Topic Sentence Outline

Transform your list of supporting points into an essay framework by writing a topic sentence (TS) outline. Topic sentences introduce each supporting paragraph in the body of the essay and announce the proof you will be presenting in that paragraph.

Following the topic sentence will be two or more sentences supporting the argument or providing the information found in the topic sentence. Here is an example of a topic sentence outline:

Sample Outline For a Short Essay on Homer[2]

General Subject: Homer's *Odyssey*

Focus 1: The importance of the home and hospitality

Focus 2: Home and hospitality in *The Odyssey*: the significance of food

Thesis: In *The Odyssey*, the frequent and detailed attention to food and the rituals surrounding it serve constantly to reinforce a central concern of the poem, the vital civilizing importance of the home.

TS 1: Throughout *The Odyssey*, we witness the way in which food taken communally can act as a way of re-energizing human beings, enabling them to cope with their distress. This, in fact, emerges as one of the most important human values in the poem. (Paragraph argues for the restorative values of food as brought out repeatedly in the poem.)

TS 2: The rituals surrounding food, especially the importance of welcoming guests to the feast and making sure everyone has enough, stress the warmth and central importance of open human interaction. (The paragraph argues the importance of hospitality as it is brought out by the references to food and feasting.)

TS 3: The occasions in which food is consumed are also moments in which the participants celebrate the artistic richness of their culture. No where else in the poem is there so much attention paid to the significance of beauty in various forms.

---

[2]This sample excerpted from the *Excellence in Literature Handbook for Writers* by Ian Johnston and Janice Campbell.

(Paragraph X argues that all the things associated with the food—the serving dishes, the entertainment, and so on—reflect important values in the culture.)

Conclusion: There is, of course, much more to the poem than the description of feasting, but we need to recognize these moments as especially important. (Paragraph restates and summarizes the central point of the argument.)

Note: Remain flexible as you write, because it is quite possible to discover another angle or better idea as you are writing. If this happens, do not worry about sticking exactly to your outline. The outline is simply a tool for organization, so you, as the author, are still in charge. Do what works.

Write the Essay

Once you have organized your ideas into an outline, it is time to begin writing. At this stage, you have thoroughly thought through the question and your ideas, and have a sturdy framework to build on. Begin writing your first draft, following the outline you have created.

Type your paper on the computer, following the formatting instructions contained in "Making Your Essay Look Good: The Basics of MLA Format," the last example in the Formats and Models chapter. At this stage, your primary concerns will be to successfully answer the essay prompt and to support your argument with relevant examples from the text. Look at the rubric in the back of the book to remind yourself of standards goals in the content, style, and mechanics of the paper.

Revise

When the draft is completed, read it aloud to yourself. This will help you pinpoint areas that seem unclear or poorly expressed. Do not skip this step! As you find things that need to be fixed, mark them and keep reading, so you do not lose the flow of the text. When you are finished, go through and fix the things you have marked. When it is as good as you can make it, turn it in.

When you receive the paper back from your writing mentor, read it aloud once again. You may be surprised to notice additional ways in which you can improve it. Refer to the evaluation rubric that you receive along with the essay, and make any improvements recommended there or in your teacher's marginal comments. Focus on fine tuning the style of the paper, including word choice, sentence fluency, and voice. You will find basic standards for these areas listed on the rubric, but your writer's handbook will help you learn even more.

Finally, when you have completed the edits recommended by your teacher, and you feel your essay meets the standards listed on the rubric, read it aloud once more. Change anything that does not sound right, check the mechanics, and when you are satisfied, turn it in.

As you follow this simple, orderly process in assignment after assignment, it will become automatic for you, and writing will become easier. By the time you reach college, you will be able to confidently tackle any writing assignment you encounter. I wish you joy in the rigorous study of the craft of writing.

Resources You May Find Helpful

The Elegant Essay Writing Lessons by Lesha Myers

Excellence in Literature Handbook for Writers

The Lost Tools of Writing from the Circe Institute

The Mind Map Book by Tony Buzan

Teaching Writing: Structure and Style from Institute for Excellence in Writing

Writing to Learn by WIlliam Zinsser

Discerning Worldview through
Literary Periods

Do you ever wonder why it is that many of history's titanic intellects managed to come to radically different conclusions? The answer is simple: If you begin your system of thought by refusing to acknowledge what you know to be true—if you start with a lie—the more brilliant and consistent you are in following that premise, the further from truth you will go.

—Tim Challies

When you are studying literature in context, literary periods can help you understand the underlying philosophy or worldview of each era. Each literary period is characterized by specific philosophical movements and historical events that affected the art, literature, and music of the day. If you have a good grasp of the assumptions that shaped each period, you will understand something of the author's worldview before you even read the book.

There are six major periods or movements in English-language literature, and each is described below with its approximate time frame. Each period has sub-periods within it, as well as overlapping characteristics. I have chosen (with permission) to adapt and use the system of categories used by Adam Andrews in *Teaching the Classics*, as I think it is an excellent, simple introduction to the subject.

Medieval (AD 500–1500)   Renaissance (1500–1660)

Neoclassical (1660–1800)   Romantic (1800–1865)

Realist (1840–1914)   Modernist (1900–1945)

Medieval (AD 500–1500)

The **Medieval** period includes the Anglo-Saxon period in the time before the 1066 Norman conquest of England, and the Middle English period after the conquest. Anglo-Saxon literature, which is based on oral storytelling, focuses on the heroic ideal which involved responsibility, leadership, loyalty, generosity, and skill in battle. After Christianity reached Britain in the seventh century, literature became overwhelmingly Christian in its themes, while still retaining its concern for the heroic ideal. The epic poem *Beowulf* is a characteristic work from this period.

The **Middle English** period was marked by a change in the purpose and audience for written literature. Anglo-Saxon works had been written by and for the aristocracy, but Middle English literature was by and for people of the lower classes. Rather than the idealized king-heroes of the Anglo-Saxon period, Middle English heroes were everyday people living in everyday situations. Christianity remained central to the medieval world, and most literature reflected this priority. This literary movement roughly coincided with the Gothic period in art and architecture. The best-known work of this period is *The Canterbury Tales* by Geoffrey Chaucer.

Renaissance (1500–1660)

The Renaissance period was a flamboyant, fervent era of exploration and expansion, characterized by several movements, including Renaissance humanism, the Protestant Reformation, and English Nationalism. Renaissance writers were concerned with classical learning, the study of the humanities (language, literature, history, art, and government), the function of religion in the world, and interest in the form and structure of human government. This literary movement roughly coincided with the baroque period in art, music, and architecture.

Authors you will recognize from this period include William Shakespeare, Edmund Spenser, John Donne, and Anne Bradstreet.

Neoclassical (1660–1800)

The Neoclassical period in literature, art, and music roughly coincided with the Age of Enlightenment. Writers in the Neoclassical period favored simplicity, clarity, restraint, regularity, and good sense, as opposed to the intricacy and boldness of the Renaissance period. Neoclassical writers sought to discover meaning in the order of things, placed society before the individual, and valued human reason over natural passions. Many of these writers were influenced by the rise of experimental science and the desire for peace and stability. Many sought to imitate the style of Roman writers such as Virgil and Ovid. The art and music of this period reflected the aesthetic values of this literary movement.

Writers of this period include Benjamin Franklin, Daniel Defoe, and Jonathan Swift.

Romantic (1800–1865)

Following the French Revolution there was general movement away from the formal literature of the Neoclassical period. Romantic art, music, and literature reflected a belief in mankind's innate goodness, equality, and potential for achievement, and strongly rejected the Neoclassical view of man as a limited being in a strictly hierarchical society. Possibly as a reaction against urbanization and other challenges of the Industrial Revolution, nature was prominently featured as a symbol of freedom of the human soul, and scenic beauty as a model for harmony. Emotion, imagination, and intuition were valued above reason and restraint. This period includes Early and Mid-Victorian literature.

Authors in this tradition include Jane Austen, Sir Walter Scott, James Fenimore Cooper, and Henry David Thoreau.

Realist (1840–1914)

Just as Romantic writers had rejected Neoclassical ideas, Realist authors, artists, and musicians rejected Romantic notions. Realists sought to portray the world and man without idealism, so their works dealt with issues such as industrialization, poverty, and inequality, sometimes focusing on the ugly or sordid. They were interested in the relationship between traditional religion, rationalist thought, and new philosophies such as Darwinism. In England, the Realist period takes place largely during the reign of Queen Victoria (1837–1901), so it includes Mid- and Late Victorian literature.

Realist writers you may know include Charles Dickens, the Brontë sisters, and Mark Twain.

One form of realism that lasted until World War II was known as **Naturalism**. Influenced by Charles Darwin's theory of evolution, Naturalist writers believed that social conditions, heredity, and environment, rather than Providence or Fate, determined man's destiny, and they often wrote about those on the fringe of society, including the uncouth and sordid. If Romantics saw the individual as a god and Realists saw him as a common man, Naturalists saw him as a helpless animal for whom free will was only an illusion.

Naturalist writers include Jack London and Stephen Crane. Edith Wharton is sometimes included in this list as well.

Modernist (1900–1945)

The dramatic changes wrought by the Industrial Revolution, Marxism, and modern scientific theories and political developments rocked the faith of twentieth-century writers. At the heart of Modernist literature is a reflection of their conviction that all the traditional structures of human life—religious, social, political, economic, and artistic—had either been destroyed or proven false. The writers' disorientation and uncertainty is often seen in the fragmented form of their fiction, and their protagonists are often aimless and frustrated rather than heroic.

Modernist authors include F. Scott Fitzgerald, Gertrude Stein, T. S. Eliot, Ernest Hemingway, Ezra Pound, and Willa Cather.

After World War II, the Modernist movement split into fragments such as Post-Modernism, Imagism, the Harlem Renaissance, Surrealism, Beat poets, Post-colonialists, and others. It is not clear which, if any, of these will prove dominant in historic hindsight. What is certain is that each of the literary periods explored here will help you understand the literature you read, in the context in which it was created.

This summary of literary periods is adapted from Teaching the Classics, *and is used courtesy of Adam Andrews. For an introduction to literary analysis and additional description of the literary periods, please see* Teaching the Classics *by Adam and Missy Andrews of The Center for Literary Education, www.CenterForLit.com.*

Using EIL in a Classroom

I have been hearing of many ways teachers are using this curriculum in classrooms and co-ops. Eventually, I hope to establish a spot on Excellence-in-Literature.com for teachers to exchange ideas and find support, but until then, here are few suggestions.

First, remember that one of the key features of EIL is the practice of college-level learning skills in addition to literary analysis. This means that students should be involved in context research and discussions about the text. The teacher or co-op leader should be functioning in the role of a facilitator, assigning areas of research and guiding discussions, rather than doing the research and lecturing on findings.

As Charlotte Mason admonished, "We err when we allow our admirable teaching to intervene between children and the knowledge their minds demand. The desire for knowledge (curiosity) is the chief agent in education: but this desire may be made powerless like an unused limb" (*A Philosophy of Education*, p. 247). She asks, "What if the devitalisation we notice in so many of our young people, keen about games but dead to things of the mind, is due to the processes carried on in our schools, to our plausible and pleasant ways of picturing, eliciting, demonstrating, illustrating, summarising, doing all those things for children which they are born with the potency to do for themselves?" (p. 237). Simply stated, learning happens when students interact with literature, not when they listen passively to a lecture.

Here are a few ideas for creating an active group learning environment:

- Introduce each module by pointing the student to the Module Focus, Literary Context, and Introduction in the text.

- Assign a context area to each student or group of students, and have them report their findings to the class.

- If the Focus Text is a poem, encourage students to listen to at least a portion of it in a professionally recorded audio version. A poem is meant to be heard, and listening will bring it to life as nothing else can.

- For each module, have students choose one passage or poem to recite or copy by hand. Recitation and copywork both aid retention of ideas and build writing skills, as both require close attention to the use of words and sequence of ideas.

- If the Focus Text is a play, always try to watch the video version. It may be best to watch it after the focus text has been read, so students will be able to appreciate subtle twists and nuances they may otherwise miss.

- Use the *Something to Think About* and *Be Sure to Notice* items as discussion starters after students have begun reading the text.

- Pull a few of the "Questions to Consider as you Read" for discussions. The most fruitful questions tend to be those that evoke an opinionated response:

  - Should [character name] do [whatever he/she is planning]? Why or why not?

  - What does it all mean? What great ideas (justice/mercy, friendship, good vs. evil, etc.) are being illustrated or embodied in the story?

  - What can you learn, or what do you think the author believes you should do or not do?

- Encourage additional research or sharing of context items not found in the EIL guide. If students find a resource they particularly like, they are welcome to submit it to me at janice@eilit.com for possible inclusion in the next edition of EIL.

- When students do an approach paper, choose some of their discussion questions to spark discussions in class. If students have chosen different key passages (this is perfectly fine), encourage them to discuss why they chose the passage they did, and why it is key.

- When students have finished the focus text, encourage discussion of how it exemplifies its literary period, and ways it may have differed from student expectations.

- If you choose to watch the movie version of a novel as part of the class, discuss how it differs from the author's creation.

- Encourage comparison of the current focus text with other works the student has read in or out of class. As they learn to discern common themes, you may find them referencing *Les Misérables*, *Merchant of Venice*, *The Little Red Hen*, and *The Lion, the Witch and the Wardrobe* in a discussion of justice and mercy. This means they are seeing through each story into the broader story beyond, and that is what it means to read with understanding.

- If you have five classroom periods each week, use one to practice what my high school used to call USSR—Uninterrupted, Sustained, Silent Reading. Many students have never been required to sit quietly for an hour and do anything, but this is an essential skill that needs to be learned, and USSR is a good way to begin. (For more on brain development and the effect of technology on language skills, I recommend *Endangered Minds* and *Failure to Connect* by Dr. Jane Healy.)

Comprehension Questions

I do not believe in using "comprehension questions" at all, except in a very limited way as practice for necessary standardized testing. I do not believe they are useful or effective, especially for high school students who should be learning to love literature, think deeply, and write thoughtfully about the literature they read.

Comprehension questions are usually trivia questions which test only student memory or the ability to catch details. Instead of helping students think deeply about the text as a whole, comprehension questions often make reading nothing more than a treasure hunt for answers. I have seen "how to study" guides that suggest students should read the comprehension questions first, then hunt for answers as they skim the story. This may be an effective strategy for timed standardized tests and may seem to be a quick and easy way to finish an assignment and move on, but it completely short circuits the learning process. Plus, it is a fast way to ruin a great book.

The writing prompts provided in EIL encourage students to thoughtfully and analytically consider something specific about the text. It is impossible to write a coherent, thoughtful paper without comprehending what you have read, so it provides a much better measure of how much the student understands about the literary work, and how well he or she writes.

Quick Guide to Excellence in Literature Learning Tools

This handy chart will help you remember some EIL basics.

Writing Process
1. Read/Research
2. Think on Paper
3. Organize
4. Write
5. Revise
p. 35

Basic Literary Periods
• Medieval
• Renaissance
• Neoclassical
• Romantic
• Realist
• Modernist
p. 41

Pencil Annotations
• Draw vertical line beside important paragraphs.
• Underline important ideas or themes.

Inside Covers
• List characters in order of appearance.
• Make a timeline of events in the story.
• Note context items to look up.
p. 28

Evaluation Criteria
• **Content**
  · ideas/concepts
  · organization
• **Style**
  · voice
  · sentence fluency
  · word choice
• Mechanics
  · conventions
  · presentation
p. 136

Formats and Models
• Approach Paper Model
• Historic/Event Approach Paper Model
• Author Profile Model
• Literature Summary Model
• Literary Analysis Model
• Poetry Analysis Model
• MLA Format Model
p. 119

MLA Page Setup
• 1" margins
• Times New Roman or similar font
• 12 point font size
p. 133

Tip: Remember to space once, not twice, after terminal punctuation (periods, question marks, etc.).

Learning Cycle
Weeks 1 & 2
• Read text and context resources.
• Do a short assignment each week.
Week 3
• Write essay or creative assignment.
• Turn in for evaluation of content and organization.
Week 4
• Revise assignment according to evaluation feedback.
• Turn in for evaluation of all standards on rubric.

Word Count Equivalent
• 250 words = one double-sided page typed in MLA format

Honors Texts
• Short Stories
• *20,000 Leagues Under the Sea* by Verne
• *The Prince and the Pauper* by Twain
• *Villette* or *Shirley* by Brontë
• *Murder in the Cathedral* by Eliot
• *Kidnapped* by Stevenson
• *1984* by Orwell *Fahrenheit 461* by Bradbury
• *A Midsummer Night's Dream* by Shakespeare
• *Pilgrim's Progress* by Bunyan

What to do for the optional Honors Track:

• Read honors texts.
• Do approach paper on one honors text.
• Write research paper.
• Take CLEP test (optional).
p. 114

Prerequisites for Success
• Have grade-level skills in language arts.

Commitment to
• read instructions;
• refer to a writer's handbook as needed;
• revise according to feedback.
p. 9

Focus Texts
• Short Stories
• *Around the World in Eighty Days* by Verne
• *A Connecticut Yankee in King Arthur's Court* by Twain
• *Jane Eyre* by Brontë
• *Pygmalion* by Shaw
• *Treasure Island* by Stevenson
• *Animal Farm* by Orwell
• *The Tempest* by Shakespeare
• *Gulliver's Travels* by Swift

Necessary Resources
• writer's handbook

Optional Resources
• dictionary
• thesaurus
• calendar for scheduling
• English notebook to store your papers
p. 18

Remember
• Follow weekly schedule for each module.
• Use the Formats and Models as a guide.
• If you have questions about grammar, style, or mechanics, consult your writer's handbook.

Websites to Remember
• Context Resources: www.Excellence-in-Literature.com
• Writing Reference at Purdue Online Lab: owl.english.purdue.edu/owl/

Module 1.1

Short Stories

When well told, a story captured the subtle movement of change.
If a novel was a map of a country, a story was the bright silver pin that marked the crossroads.

—Ann Patchett

Focus Text

In most modules, your focus text will be a single longer work, such as a novel or play. In this module, however, you will work with several short stories. In the first assignment, you will learn to write an approach paper while enjoying "The White Heron." In the second exercise, you will briefly analyze literary elements in several short stories, so that you will be better able to recognize them in the longer books you will study throughout the year. Finally, you will write a short compare/contrast essay.

Be sure to use complete sentences to express your ideas. Remember to put your name, the date, the class name, and the module title in the top left corner of each assignment you turn in. For essays or stories, you should also copy the assignment prompt just below this information so that you will have it handy as you are writing, and your evaluator will know exactly which question you are answering.

Focus Text for Part One

A White Heron by Sarah Orne Jewett (1849–1909)

https://excellence-in-literature.com/]a-white-heron-by-sarah-orne-jewett

Context Reading for Part One

You will find a clickable list of the links in this chapter on the EIL website:

https://excellence-in-literature.com/curriculum-user-content/e1-context-resources/eil-1-1-short-stories-context/

Introduction and chronology of Sarah Orne Jewett's life (click on "Biography" link to learn more about her life):

https://excellence-in-literature.com/sarah-orne-jewett-biography/

http://www.public.coe.edu/~theller/soj/bio/intro.html

If you would like to listen to an audio version of the story, you will find a recording at:

https://excellence-in-literature.com/a-white-heron-audio/

Focus Texts for Part Two

The Diamond Necklace by Guy de Maupassant (1850–1893)

https://excellence-in-literature.com/the-diamond-necklace

The Ransom of Red Chief by O. Henry (1862-1910)

https://excellence-in-literature.com/the-ransom-of-red-chief-by-o-henry

A Worn Path by Eudora Welty (1909–2001)

https://excellence-in-literature.com/a-worn-path-by-eudora-welty

The Secret Life of Walter Mitty by James Thurber (1894–1961)

http://goo.gl/1RlBoW or

http://www.newyorker.com/archive/1939/03/18/390318fi_fiction_thurber?currentPage=all

The Purloined Letter by Edgar Allen Poe (1809–1849)

https://excellence-in-literature.com/the-purloined-letter-by-edgar-allan-poe

Honors Texts

If you wish to follow the honors option, use an encyclopedia to read biographical information about each of the focus text authors in this chapter. You will also need to read at least one additional short story of your choice by each of the authors studied. You can find more short stories by these authors in a short story anthology from your library, or you may search online. Gutenberg.org is a good source for older stories by these authors.

Literary Period

These short stories were written in the nineteenth and twentieth centuries; therefore, they represent a range of literary periods from Romantic (Poe) to Realist and Modernist. As you read each story, look back at the description of the literary period in the *Discerning Worldview Through Literary Periods* chapter, and see if you can observe ways in which each story fits its period.

Module Focus

- Learn to use your *Excellence in Literature* book, along with your writer's handbook, and other reference materials to complete assignments independently.
- Learn to write an approach paper.
- Discover or review the five elements of fiction—plot, theme, characterization, setting, and style—in five great short stories.
- Write a basic compare/contrast essay.

Introduction

We are using short stories for this first module, because it is easy to see each of the five elements of fiction (plot, theme, characterization, setting, and style) when everything happens in fewer than 2000 words. Two of the stories are humorous, at least three have surprise endings, and one is considered a regional human interest story. These are some of my favorite short story authors—I hope you enjoy them!

Something to think about . . .

In some of the stories, the main character's name seems very important, while in other stories, you scarcely notice it. Does this change the way you feel about the character? When the author chooses a name such Phoenix (a phoenix is a mythical bird with glorious plumage, who lives about 500 years, then burns on a funeral pyre and is reborn for another life cycle) for the character of an elderly, impoverished black lady, what do you think she wants to convey about this character?

Be sure to notice . . .

Character names very often have an allusive meaning (see the glossary or a dictionary if you're not sure what that means). Notice names as you read, and in light of the story, consider why the author may have chosen the name.

Context Resources

Context Resources for "The Diamond Necklace"

Video

https://excellence-in-literature.com/the-diamond-necklace-audio

Context Resources for "The Ransom of Red Chief"

Video

https://excellence-in-literature.com/the-ransom-of-red-chief-dramatized

Context Resources for "A Worn Path"

This video dramatization of "A Worn Path" may help you understand the story more vividly.

https://excellence-in-literature.com/
dramatization-of-eudora-weltys-story-a-worn-path

Dr. Randy Laist of Goodwin College provides a helpful analysis of "A Worn Path." You may not understand all you read in this analysis, but it will show you new ways to think about literature.

https://excellence-in-literature.com/
dramatization-of-eudora-weltys-story-a-worn-path

Context Resources for "The Secret Life of Walter Mitty"

A graphic organizer can help you see the structure of the real and imaginary elements in this story.

http://www.webenglishteacher.com/msb/mitty/mittygoPDF.pdf

Context Resources for "The Purloined Letter"

Video

https://excellence-in-literature.com/
dramatization-of-eudora-weltys-story-a-worn-path

This PDF graphic organizer will help you see the various elements of the story.

http://etc.usf.edu/lit2go/pdf/student_activity/5357/5357-1.pdf

The Authors' Life and Historical Context

Use your encyclopedia to learn a little bit about each author and the time in which
he or she lived. An author can be influenced by a particular place or literary
movement, or by personal tragedy, triumph, illness, or other life circumstances.
Pay special attention to events in the author's life that may have influenced the
type of stories he or she wrote.

Places to Go (optional, of course!)

Sarah Orne Jewett's home has been transformed into a museum in South Berwick,
Maine.

http://www.historicnewengland.org/historic-properties/homes/
sarah-orne-jewett-house

Eudora Welty's home in Jackson, Mississippi is now a museum. You may enjoy visiting this historic literary house. More information is available at:

https://eudorawelty.org/visit/

The Museum of Edgar Allen Poe is located in an old stone house in downtown Rich-
mond, Virginia, near the location where Poe lived.

https://www.poemuseum.org

You may take a virtual tour of the historic home of Guy de Maupassant, located in
Etreatat, France. If you are studying French, you may choose to read the site
information in that language.

http://www.houseofmaupassant.com

James Thurber's home in Columbus, Ohio, is open for tours. The website, subtitled
"where laughter, learning, and literature meet," offers a variety of educational
programs.

http://www.thurberhouse.org

The O. Henry Museum is hosted by the government of Austin, Texas. The website
features a biography and events, including a Pun-Off contest.

http://www.austintexas.gov/department/o-henry-museum

Assignment Schedule

Week 1

Preliminary Reading: Before you begin reading the stories and writing your assignments for this module, you need to read through the first few chapters of this book, if you have not already done so, and look at the writing samples in the "Formats and Models" chapter as well. You also need to become familiar with your writer's handbook, and to read all the way through this module so that you will know what you will be doing for the next four weeks.

Do the preliminary readings, then read *A White Heron* and the context readings (above). Write an approach paper on *A White Heron*, using the instructions and samples in the Formats and Models chapter. In addition to the context links I have provided, you may use other resources such as your encyclopedia, the library, and quality Internet resources to help you complete this assignment.

Weeks 2 and 3

Read each of the assigned stories, one per day.

Review "How to Read a Book," looking up unfamiliar terms in the Glossary, so that you can recognize the five elements of fiction.

Follow the Literature Summary Model in the Formats and Models chapter to write a Literature Summary for each story. There are five stories, and ten school days in which to work, so you will probably spend two days on each story—one day in reading; one day in writing.

Week 4

Monday-Wednesday: Draft a 300-word paper on the topic below. I recommend that you follow the writing process outlined in the "How to Write an Essay" chapter, consulting the models in the Formats and Models chapter and your writer's handbook as needed.

Model: Literary Analysis Essay and MLA Format Model

Prompt: Choose two of the assigned stories, and write an essay comparing and contrasting ways in which the selected works are similar/different in one or two of the following areas: plot, theme, characterization, setting, and style.

For additional help, use your writer's handbook or refer to the "How to Write a Compare/Contrast Essay " article at the first URL below, and see a model at the second URL:

https://excellence-in-literature.com/how-to-write-a-compare-contrast-essay/

https://excellence-in-literature.com/sample-compare-contrast-essay/

Consider using a graphic organizer such as the Venn diagram to help organize your thoughts before you write your essay. Your writer's handbook may have instructions and models of many types of graphic organizers, or you may view some at my Pinterest board.

http://www.pinterest.com/janicecampbell/graphic-organizers/

Edit your draft. Be sure your thesis is clear to the reader and that your essay is well-organized and free from mechanical errors. Use the evaluation rubric in the "Tips for Evaluating Writing" chapter to check your work.

Thursday: Turn in the draft on Thursday, so your writing mentor can evaluate it using the Content standards (Ideas/Concepts and Organization) on the rubric.

Friday: Use the feedback on the rubric along with the writing mentor's comments to revise your paper. Before turning in the final draft, be sure you have addressed any issues marked on the evaluation rubric, and verify that the thesis is clear and your essay is well-organized. Use your writer's handbook to check grammar or punctuation so that your essay will be free from mechanical errors. Turn in the essay at the end of the week so that the writing mentor can use the evaluation rubric in the "How to Evaluate" chapter to check your work.

Module 1.2

Around the World in Eighty Days by Jules Verne (1828–1905)

Whatever one man is capable of conceiving, other men will be able to achieve.

—Jules Verne

Focus Text

Around the World in Eighty Days by Jules Verne

Honors Text

20,000 Leagues Under the Sea by Jules Verne

Literary Period

Romantic, Science Fiction

Module Focus

You will learn about the Victorian fascination with travel, exotic lands and peoples, and the concept of the shrinking world.

Introduction

The French writer, Jules Verne, wrote science and adventure stories that seemed fantastic to his 19th-century contemporaries, but have proven surprisingly prophetic. In this module, we will study one of Verne's best-known stories, *Around the World in Eighty Days*. I think you will enjoy following Phileas Fogg and his valet, Passepartout, as they race against a deadline in order to win a wager.

Something to think about . . .

It was during the Victorian era that travel became increasingly possible for many people. Railroads reached far into places that seemed exotic, and ships sailed regularly for faraway lands. Jules Verne looked beyond what was happening, and created novels that no longer seemed absurdly impossible. If man could travel around the world in eighty days, why couldn't he journey to the center of the earth or live 20,000 leagues under the sea?

Be sure to notice . . .

Jules Verne has chosen a special format for his chapter titles. Each title begins with "In which . . ." and offers a mini-preview of the chapter. What do you think might be the purpose of this type of title?

Context Resources

You will find a clickable list of the links in this chapter on the EIL website:

https://excellence-in-literature.com/curriculum-user-content/e1-context-resources/eil-1-2-verne-context/

Readings

Jules Verne wrote very few short stories, but this one, "In the Year 2889," was commissioned in 1889 by an editor who wanted a story about the United States as it would be, one thousand years later. It is fascinating to see how many of Verne's ideas have become reality.

https://excellence-in-literature.com/in-the-year-2889-by-jules-verne-2

If you would like to read more of Verne's works, you may do so for free at this site.

http://www.readprint.com/author-85/Jules-Verne

These brief quotes are an interesting way to help you get acquainted with Verne and his works.

https://www.brainyquote.com/quotes/authors/j/jules_verne.html

The Author's Life

Jules Verne: The Biography of an Imagination by George H. Waltz, Jr. or

Jules Verne: The Man Who Invented the Future by Franz Born or any middle-grade Verne biography from your library.

What did Verne have to say about his own life? In this 1894 interview, R. H. Sherard interviews Jules Verne about his life and work.

https://excellence-in-literature.com/jules-verne-at-home-1894-interview-by-sherard

If you find Verne especially interesting, you may also enjoy *Jules Verne: An Exploratory Biography* by Herbert R. Lottman (1997)

Poetry

Jules Verne wrote several poems that were included in his short stories and novels. This website shows the excerpts of some of his poems in the original French, plus some English translations.

http://verne.garmtdevries.nl/en/poetry/ownpoems.html

Audio

There is an excellent audiobook version of *Around the World in Eighty Days* narrated by Alan Munro. It is available at Audible.com or Amazon.

http://amzn.to/2sTEoJB

Alternatively, you may listen to an amateur recording at Librivox:

http://librivox.org/around-the-world-in-eighty-days-by-jules-verne-2/

Music

Listen to music from the 1956 movie score by Victor Young. This site has a music player with lyrical versions by singers such as Bing Crosby and Frank Sinatra:

http://jv.gilead.org.il/around.html

Jules Verne is mentioned in the lyrics of this song, "Globe Trotting Nelly Bly".

http://www.traditionalmusic.co.uk/old-time-music/003930.HTM

Video

I have not seen any of the movie versions of *Around the World in 80 Days*, so please consult a reliable movie review site to find a suitable production. Here is a trailer from the 1956 movie:

https://excellence-in-literature.com//
trailer-for-around-the-world-in-80-days-1956-film

Visual Arts

Jules Verne was featured in various art forms, including photographs, cartoons, sculpture, and more. Here are a few samples.

http://www.julesverne.ca/jvjulesverne.html

Learn more about the illustrators of Verne's *Voyages Extraordinaires*.

http://jv.gilead.org.il/evans/illustr/

International Interest

These websites demonstrate the remarkable amount of international interest in Jules Verne. They are well worth exploring in order to gain a better understanding of the man and his era.

Garmt de Vries-Uiterweerd, a noted Jules Verne collector, has put together many Verne resources and links, plus a quiz and context materials. Browse the site: note the maps from original Verne editions (listed under "Cartography") and links to other excellent Verne resources (some are not in English). If you study French, you may want to read this resource in French by clicking on "Français" in the upper right hand corner of any page.

http://verne.garmtdevries.nl/en/

http://verne.garmtdevries.nl/en/voyages/world.cgi (interactive map of the journey)

Another Jules Verne site by Canadian collector, Andrew Nash, includes numerous images of vintage book covers and illustrations, links, and a family tree. This site is nicely organized, and the vintage illustrations are especially interesting.

http://www.julesverne.ca/index.html

Zvi Har'El's Jules Verne Collection is another must-not-miss resource, with some unique links and a comprehensive list of available Hebrew translations of Verne's works.

http://jv.gilead.org.il/

Places to Go

The home of Jules Verne is now a museum in Nantes, France. This French-language site offers information and photos.

http://www.nantes.fr/julesverne/acc_4.htm

Jules Verne's tomb in Amiens, France, features a very odd gravestone:

http://www.julesverne.ca/jvtomb.html

If you would like to visit the London locations of Philias Fogg's home and club, you might want to begin with a look at Garmt de Vries-Uiterweerd's essay about his experience in visiting these sites.

http://verne.garmtdevries.nl/en/london/

Assignment Schedule

Week 1

Read and explore context materials, and begin reading focus text. Follow the model in the Formats and Models chapter to write an Author Profile. Be sure to refer to your writer's handbook if you have questions about grammar, structure, or style.

Week 2

Write an approach paper, using the instructions and samples in the Formats and Models chapter. In addition to the context links I have provided, you may use other resources such as your encyclopedia, the library, and quality Internet resources to help you complete this assignment.

Week 3

Watch the video (optional).

Begin drafting a 500-word paper on one of the topics below. I recommend that you follow the writing process outlined in the "How to Write an Essay" chapter, consulting the models in the Formats and Models chapter and your writer's handbook as needed.

Model: Literary Analysis Essay and MLA Format Model

Prompt: Phileas Fogg's valet, Passepartout, is a major source of comedy in the story. Do his actions help or hinder Fogg on his journey? To support your argument, discuss specific events in the story, using appropriate quotes from the text to illustrate your point.

Alternate Assignment

Write the story in the form of a news article reporting on Fogg's journey. Tell the story with colorful details, making sure that your reader will finish the tale with a vivid understanding of the characters and events. Make this at least 500 words or as long as necessary in order to tell a good tale. Use the journalistic format shown at:

https://excellence-in-literature.com/journalism-story-structure-by-mark-grabowski/

Turn in the draft at the end of the week, so your writing mentor can evaluate it using the Content standards (Ideas/Concepts and Organization) on the rubric.

Week 4

Use the feedback on the rubric, along with the writing mentor's comments to revise your paper. Before turning in the final draft, be sure you have addressed any issues marked on the evaluation rubric, and verify that the thesis is clear and your essay is well-organized. Use your writer's handbook to check grammar or punctuation so that your essay will be free from mechanical errors. Turn in the essay at the end of the week so that the writing mentor can use the evaluation rubric in the "How to Evaluate" chapter to check your work.

Module 1.3

A Connecticut Yankee in King Arthur's Court
by Mark Twain (1835–1910)

The rain . . . falls upon the just and the unjust alike;
a thing which would not happen if I were superintending the rain's affairs.
No, I would rain softly and sweetly on the just, but if I caught a sample of the unjust outdoors
I would drown him.

— Mark Twain

Focus Text

A Connecticut Yankee in King Arthur's Court by Mark Twain OR *Joan of Arc* by Mark Twain

Honors Text

The Prince and the Pauper by Mark Twain

Literary Period

Romantic

Module Focus

The author's use of irony and framed narrative in an entertaining story, designed to vividly convey the author's viewpoint on serious issues.

Introduction

American novelist Samuel Clemens is best known by his pseudonym, Mark Twain. His tales combine humor, irony, and a keen sense of observation.

In this module, we will read *A Connecticut Yankee In King Arthur's Court*, one of the few Twain novels in which the main action takes place outside the United States. The protagonist Hank Morgan, a Connecticut Yankee, receives a blow to the head and is transported back to the time of King Arthur, where he tries to improve medieval systems with Yankee ingenuity. Twain's satire is both funny and thought provoking.

Something to think about . . .

Twain wrote this novel about twenty-five years after the Civil War. What issues do you see in *Connecticut Yankee* that may be related to Twain's perception of the Civil War? Can you determine Twain's view on the issue of slavery?

Be sure to notice . . .

This story is told as a framed narrative, which is a story within a story. The narrative of Hank's adventures in the medieval world is framed by the story of his accident and recovery. This literary device appears in other famous classical works such as *The Canterbury Tales* by Geoffrey Chaucer. In this ancient book, the stories of the individual pilgrims are framed by the story of their journey to Canterbury. As you read, think about how the framing story affects your perception of the central narrative.

Context Resources

You will find a clickable list of the links in this chapter on the EIL website:

https://excellence-in-literature.com/curriculum-user-content/e1-context-resources/eil-1-3-mark-twain-context/

The Author's Life

There are so many good books about Mark Twain that it is hard to choose just one! You may want to begin with the website, and then read the short biography of your choice.

https://excellence-in-literature.com/mark-twain-bio-1911-eb

The official website for Mark Twain contains a brief biography, photos, quotes about and by the author.

http://www.cmgww.com/historic/twain/

http://www.marktwainhouse.org/man/biography_main.php

Mark Twain: America's Humorist, Dreamer, Prophet by Clinton Cox (or other short biography available at your local library)

The Courtship of Olivia Langdon and Mark Twain by Susan K. Harris

The Autobiography of Mark Twain by Mark Twain

Mr. Clemens and Mark Twain: A Biography by Justin Kaplan

Mark Twain: An Illustrated Biography by Geoffrey C. Ward

Poetry

"The Idylls of the King" by Alfred, Lord Tennyson: This epic poem was extremely popular during Mark Twain's lifetime, and may have influenced his writing of *A Connecticut Yankee*. Read the section, "The Coming of Arthur" and any others that appeal to you. It is included in many poetry anthologies, or you can read it at the link below:

https://excellence-in-literature.com/
idylls-of-the-king-written-by-alfred-lord-tennyson

Mark Twain did not claim to be a poet, but he did write a few poems. Be sure to read the following poems at:

https://excellence-in-literature.com/poetry-by-mark-twain

- "A Sweltering Day In Australia"
- "Genius"
- "Ode to Stephen Dowling Bots"
- "The Aged Pilot Man"
- "Those Annual Bills"
- "To Jennie"

Audio

There is some evidence to suggest that Thomas Edison recorded Mark Twain's voice on wax cylinder. That recording is no longer available, but you may listen to interesting re-creations of some of Twain's lectures at:

http://classiclit.about.com/od/marktwainfaqs/f/faq_mtwain_voic.htm

Audiobook of *A Connecticut Yankee In King Arthur's Court* narrated by Stuart Langton

http://amzn.to/2tNKpaZ

Amateur recording from Librivox:

http://librivox.org/a-connecticut-yankee-in-king-arthurs-court-by-mark-twain/

Music

Mr. Mark Twain: The Musical (2009) You may listen online to brief samples of songs from the musical:

http://amzn.to/2seNrTz

Mark Twain's Mississippi music page at the University of Illinois offers recordings of some of the historic songs of Twain's time.

http://twain.lib.niu.edu/music

The Raging Canal: Listen to this popular canal song of the 1800's, which inspired *The Aged Pilot Man*, a parody by Mark Twain.

http://www.traditionalmusic.co.uk/song-midis/Raging_Canal.html

Video

The Adventures of Mark Twain (1944 and 1985)

https://excellence-in-literature.com/the-adventures-of-mark-twain

Mark Twain (2001) A television biography directed by Ken Burns.

A Connecticut Yankee In King Arthur's Court was filmed for television in 1989, but I have not seen it. If your library has a copy, it may be worth watching.

Visual Arts

Here are a few images of Mark Twain, including one of him playing the piano for his wife, Clara Clemens and a friend. It is interesting to look at the backgrounds in the photos to see how he lived.

https://excellence-in-literature.com/mark-twain-images

Steamboat Times depicts "a pictorial history of the Mississippi steamboating era," complete with many interesting photos of Mark Twain and his family:

http://steamboattimes.com/mark_twain_gallery_1.html

Other Resources

Mark Twain's Mississippi offers songs about the Mississippi River from 1830-1890, as well as maps, and other resources that "try to build a larger image of what the Mississippi Valley meant to people in Mark Twain's time; how these meanings influenced his own interpretation of the place, and, finally, how his vision has fed into the many we hold today."

http://twain.lib.niu.edu/

"A Curious Pleasure Excursion" is a humorous short piece by Mark Twain, written in response to a comet scare:

https://excellence-in-literature.com/a-curious-pleasure-excursion-by-mark-twain

At this University of Virginia site, read a brief, interesting article on "King Arthur's Court In Mark Twain's America," and try out Twain's Memory Game.

http://etext.virginia.edu/railton/yankee/mtcamlot.html

Twain was ultimately quotable, and you will enjoy browsing through this site that contains some of his most memorable quotes, plus newspaper and magazine articles, as well as quirky items such as a photo of Susy Clemens' headstone, photos of other men that Twain was often mistaken for, and more.

http://www.twainquotes.com/

Take an interesting virtual tour of Twain's unique Hartford, Connecticut house, where he lived and worked from 1874-1891.

https://excellence-in-literature.com/mark-twain-house-video

Ken Burns created a film about Mark Twain, which was shown on PBS in 2002. This companion site includes an interesting, interactive scrapbook about the life of Mark Twain.

http://www.pbs.org/marktwain/

Assignment Schedule

Week 1

Begin reading the focus work. Be sure to consider the questions below as you read.

- What are Hank Morgan's beliefs about superstition? Think about how and why he uses superstition in the story, and what he accomplishes by doing so.

- How does Hank Morgan view religion? Do you think his beliefs reflect Twain's? Why or why not?

- How does Hank use his power? Does he use it for the benefit of the people or for his own glory, or a combination of the two?

- There are two distinct views of knighthood in the novel. Consider these two views, and how they may reflect Twain's views of honor, especially in light of the rhetoric of the Civil War.

- Morgan le Fay plays an interesting role in the novel. How does she reflect Twain's view of the evils of the age?

Follow the model in the Formats and Models chapter to write an Author Profile. Be sure to refer to your writer's handbook if you have questions about grammar, structure, or style.

Week 2

Write an approach paper, using the instructions and samples in the Formats and Models chapter. In addition to the context links I have provided, you may use other resources such as your encyclopedia, the library, and quality Internet resources to help you complete this assignment.

As an alternate assignment, you may draw a graphic storyline of the major events in the book. This would be styled like a graphic novel or comic book, with one or more two-page spreads per scene. In addition to the context links provided, you may use other resources such as your encyclopedia, the library, and quality Internet resources to complete this assignment.

Week 3

Begin drafting a 500-word paper on the topic below. I recommend that you follow the writing process outlined in the "How to Write an Essay" chapter, consulting the models in the Formats and Models chapter and your writer's handbook as needed.

Model: Literary Analysis Essay and MLA Format Model

Prompt: Although this book is a humorous time-travel story, Twain addresses a number of serious social issues through the Connecticut Yankee's experiences. Consider how Hank Morgan's story expresses Twain's views on monarchy versus democracy, slavery and/or serfdom, or technology versus tradition. Choose one of these issues and show how Twain used Morgan's experiences to express his views and how these views reflect the values of America during his time.

Week 4

Use the feedback on the rubric, along with the writing mentor's comments to revise your paper. Before turning in the final draft, be sure you have addressed any issues marked on the evaluation rubric, and verify that the thesis is clear and your essay is well-organized. Use your writer's handbook to check grammar or punctuation so that your essay will be free from mechanical errors. Turn in the essay at the end of the week so that the writing mentor can use the evaluation rubric in the "How to Evaluate" chapter to check your work.

Module 1.4

Jane Eyre by Charlotte Brontë (1816–1855)

Prejudices, it is well known, are most difficult to eradicate from the heart whose soil has never been loosened or fertilized by education; they grow firm there, firm as weeds among stones.

—Charlotte Brontë

Focus Text

Jane Eyre by Charlotte Brontë (Ignatius Critical Edition)

Honors Text

Villette or *Shirley* by Charlotte Brontë

Literary Period

Romantic

Module Focus

You will observe Brontë's creation of a new type of heroine, and look at her unique blend of the traditions of Gothic novels with the novel of society and manners (see "gothic" and "manners" in the Glossary).

Introduction

With the creation of Jane Eyre, Charlotte Brontë introduced a new type of heroine to the English novel tradition. Jane's strengths were not beauty nor charm, but intelligence and integrity. Like Brontë herself, Jane was small, plain, and socially powerless, yet she makes courageous choices and demonstrates inner strength.

As you read *Jane Eyre*, you will recognize elements from the Gothic novel, as well as elements from novels of society and manners. Once you have read about the author's life, you may understand how she was able to think so creatively, even in a society that did not expect women to contribute to the field of literature.

Something to think about . . .

Many novels in the Victorian era dealt with the sad plight of orphans or the horrors of boarding schools and poorhouses. In Brontë's portrayal of Lowood School, what do you think she wants the reader to feel about institutions like this? Do you think she admires the people who run them?

Be sure to notice . . .

Charlotte Brontë has Jane narrate her own story. How does this first-person narration affect the way you view Jane and how you feel about her experiences?

Context Resources

You will find a clickable list of the links in this chapter on the EIL website:

https://excellence-in-literature.com/curriculum-user-content/e1-context-resources/eil-1-4-charlotte-bronte-context/

The Author's Life

Read about the author in any of the following books or others you may find at your library.

Charlotte Brontë by Jane Sellars (The British Library *Writer's Lives* series by Oxford University Press)–This brief biography is very well done, with many illustrations. I recommend it highly.

The Oxford Companion to the Brontës by Christine Alexander and Margaret Smith

The Brontës: A Life In Letters by Juliet Barker

The Life of Charlotte Brontë by Elizabeth Gaskell

Brontë Country offers information about the Brontë's home, village, and surrounding area; the many photos, links, and other interesting tidbits will help you place Charlotte Brontë into geographical and historical context.

http://www.bronte-country.com/welcome.html

A very brief biography and a few famous quotes by Charlotte Brontë.

http://brontec.thefreelibrary.com/

The Victorian Web's Charlotte Brontë overview includes a brief biography, a list of her works, essays on relevant themes, and much more.

http://www.victorianweb.org/authors/bronte/cbronte/bronteov.html

Poetry

We do not usually think of Charlotte Brontë as a poet, but she wrote a number of interesting poems. You can read several here:

https://excellence-in-literature.com/charlotte-bronte-poetry/

Audio

Unabridged audiobook, narrated by Andrea Giordani:

http://amzn.to/2u9WN4p

Alternate amateur readings:

http://www.gutenberg.org/etext/23077 or

http://librivox.org/jane-eyre-by-charlotte-bront/

Download the audio book of *Villette* by Charlotte Brontë for free at:

http://www.gutenberg.org/etext/21181

Music

As the daughter of an Anglican clergyman, Charlotte Brontë would have been familiar with the church music of the time.

http://excellence-in-literature.com/intro-to-lit/e1-resources/
music-the-bronte-sisters-may-have-known

Jane Eyre: The Musical (2000) by Paul Gordon

Read a review of the musical:

http://www.tracksounds.com/reviews/janeeyre.htm

You can listen to clips from the musical at Amazon.com:

http://goo.gl/UA6isJ

Video

The classic black and white *Jane Eyre* movie (1944) starring Orson Welles, Joan Fontaine, and Margaret O'Brien can often be found at the library. Here is a trailer:

https://excellence-in-literature.com/jane-eyre-trailer/

Jane Eyre (1983) BBC 11-part miniseries starring Timothy Dalton, Zelah Clarke, and Sian Pattenden .

Visual Arts

Do not miss this fascinating description of Jane Eyre's three paintings and their symbolic meanings.

https://excellence-in-literature.com/
jane-eyres-three-paintings-biblical-warnings-greek-legends-by-peter-bolt

Places to Go

Visit the Brontë Parsonage Museum and Brontë Society website for information about the entire Brontë family, including a family history, individual profiles, a chronology, and many interesting links (listed under "Library"); there is even a link to rent, for a short stay, the cottage where Charlotte Brontë's husband Arthur Bell Nichols lived before their marriage. Be sure to read at least three posts from the blog.

Website: http://www.bronte.org.uk/

Blog: http://bronteparsonage.blogspot.com/

It is interesting to read the inscription on the family vault where Charlotte Brontë was buried with the Brontë family.

http://theliterarycemetery.blogspot.com/2009/03/grave-charlotte-bronte-1816-1855.
html

Assignment Schedule

Week 1

Begin reading focus work and context resources. Think about the following questions as you read.

- Think about the relationship between the character of Jane Eyre and the atmosphere of her various homes—Gateshead, Lowood, Thornfield, Moor House/Marsh End, and Ferndean. How does Charlotte Brontë use each home setting to portray Jane's position in life and her level of personal freedom and happiness?
- Brontë has Jane describe several of her paintings and drawings. What do these reveal about Jane's creativity, imagination, and personality?
- Consider the character of Edward Rochester in contrast to St. John Rivers. Neither character is entirely appealing as a romantic hero. Why do you think Charlotte Brontë chose to portray them in this way, and how did she make one seem a more sympathetic character than the other?

Follow the model in the Formats and Models chapter to write an Author Profile. Be sure to refer to your writer's handbook if you have questions about grammar, structure, or style.

Week 2

Finish novel.

Assume the character of Jane Eyre, and write three journal entries describing three important events in her life, and how she may have felt about them. Remember to write in character, and to use appropriate language and vocabulary for Jane's age and circumstances. Your model will be Jane's voice in the novel.

Week 3

Finish context works and begin drafting a 500-word paper on the topic below. I recommend that you follow the writing process outlined in the "How to Write an Essay" chapter, consulting the models in the Formats and Models chapter and your writer's handbook as needed.

Model: Literary Analysis Essay and MLA Format Model

Prompt: Secrets play a large role in *Jane Eyre*. Describe two of the most important plot secrets that provide turning points in the novel, and explain how they help to generate suspense or introduce conflict or resolution. Be sure to use specific quotes from the text to support your argument.

Turn in the draft at the end of the week, so your writing mentor can evaluate it using the Content standards (Ideas/Concepts and Organization) on the rubric.

Week 4

Use the feedback on the rubric along with the writing mentor's comments to revise your paper. Before turning in the final draft, be sure you have addressed any issues marked on the evaluation rubric and verify that the thesis is clear and your essay is well-organized. Use your writer's handbook to check grammar or punctuation so that your essay will be free from mechanical errors. Turn in the essay at the end of the week so that the writing mentor can use the evaluation rubric in the "How to Evaluate" chapter to check your work.

Module 1.5

Pygmalion by George Bernard Shaw (1856–1950)

A life spent making mistakes is not only more honorable,
but more useful than a life spent doing nothing.

—George Bernard Shaw

Focus Text

Pygmalion by George Bernard Shaw

Honors Text

Murder in the Cathedral by T. S. Eliot–An excellent drama in the style of a Greek Tragedy, written by a Shaw contemporary. As you read this, compare Eliot's writing style and tone with Shaw's.

Literary Period

Realist

Module Focus

In this module, you will learn to see elements of continuity in different literary forms.

Introduction

Many modern novels and plays borrow themes, plot lines, or characters from older works. In *Pygmalion*, Irish playwright George Bernard Shaw borrows the title and general plot line from an ancient Greek legend told in Ovid's *Metamorphoses*. The legend has been adapted and updated many times over the years. Probably the most memorable recent adaptation of *Pygmalion* is the musical comedy, *My Fair Lady*.

Something to think about . . .

Eliza's social class and level of education is reflected in her speech. Higgins says, "It's "ow" and "garn" that keeps her in her place; not her wretched clothes and dirty face." Consider the types of speech you hear in the media and in your home, as well as what you read in books, newspapers, and personal correspondence. How does each type of speech reflect the speaker's place in life? How can accurate, graceful communication affect a speaker's reception by others, and his or her chance for success in life?

Be sure to notice . . .

As you study the various transformations of the ancient legend in this module, and write your own creative work, notice that the theme and general plot line of the story will remain constant, while the setting and characters can be completely transformed without losing the essence of the tale. If you had to rank the literary elements of plot, theme, characterization, setting, and style in order of importance, based on what you have noticed in this module, how would you rank them?

Context Resources

You will find a clickable list of the links in this chapter on the EIL website:

https://excellence-in-literature.com/curriculum-user-content/e1-context-resources/
eil-1-5-george-bernard-shaw-context/

Readings

Coolidge, Olivia. *Greek Myths*: Boston, c. 1942 Houghton-Mifflin Co.

"Legend of Pygmalion and Galatea" from *A Book of Myths: Selections from Bulfinch's Age of Fable* (MacMillan Publishing Co., New York) c. 1942. This can also be viewed online at:

https://excellence-in-literature.com/
pygmalion-and-galatea-legend-told-by-thomas-bulfinch

"How to Write a Popular Play"–Do not miss this interesting and useful essay by George Bernard Shaw:

https://excellence-in-literature.com/
how-to-write-a-popular-play-by-george-bernard-shaw

If you would like to read or perform *Pygmalion* in a group, you may download free copies of the play at Gutenberg.org:

http://www.gutenberg.org/etext/3825

Famous quotes by George Bernard Shaw:

http://www.elise.com/q/quotes/shawquotes.htm

The Author's Life

George Bernard Shaw by G. K. Chesterton (available from the library, Gutenberg. org, or from Amazon.com) Chesterton, a Christian writer and friend of GBS, provides a critique of Shaw's works.

http://www.gutenberg.org/ebooks/19535

Shaw and Chesterton were intellectual titans of their age, and they had a very interesting relationship. You can get a sense of their personalities and writing styles in this brief video.

https://excellence-in-literature.com/the-humor-of-g-b-shaw-and-g-k-chesterton/

"Chesterton-Shaw Debate Speaks to the Present Crisis" reports on a debate reenactment between friends. While this is an optional resource, it provides a more detailed look at these two men, their differences, and the ways in which they used intelligent humor to make their points.

http://www.ewtn.com/library/ISSUES/CHESSHAW.TXT

Shaw won the 1925 Nobel Prize in Literature. You may read his biography at the Nobel site, then click on the header entitled *The Nobel Prize in Literature 1925* to reach the link for the presentation speech, which will provide you with a more vivid picture of his personality and work. Very interesting!

http://nobelprize.org/nobel_prizes/literature/laureates/1925/shaw.html

Britannica offers a brief, nicely organized biography of Shaw, followed by a list of additional reading, links, and interesting quotes. Do not miss the videos (the first one is a charming clip of Shaw speaking about the novelty of modern technology, and it provides a nice introduction to his speaking voice), as well as the images of Shaw, on the left side bar.

http://www.britannica.com/EBchecked/topic/539048/George-Bernard-Shaw

Another brief, interesting biography by Cary M. Mazer, University of Pennsylvania, can be found at:

https://excellence-in-literature.com/bernard-shaw-a-brief-biography

George Bernard Shaw: His Life and Works, a Critical Biography by Archibald Henderson is an interesting biography with good photographs and a genealogical chart. You may find it in your local library, or view a digitized copy at:

https://excellence-in-literature.com/
george-bernard-shaw-a-biography-by-archibald-henderson

Poetry

Although George Bernard Shaw is not known for poetry, some of his best friends and contemporaries were. As you read, remember that these writers, along with Shaw, were known for great intellect, superb writing, and a keen sense of humor. Read the Belloc poems, and selections from the other two books (you should be able to find them at your library).

Hilaire Belloc

- "Child! Do not throw this book about"
- "Jim, Who ran away from his Nurse, and was eaten by a Lion"

http://excellence-in-literature.com/poetry-2/poetry-by-hilaire-belloc

Collected Nonsense and Light Verse by G. K. Chesterton

- One of these delightful poems is entitled: "Irresponsible Outbreak of One Who, Having Completed a Book of Enormous Length on the Poet Chaucer, Feels Himself Freed from all Bonds of Intellectual Self-Respect and Proposes to do no Work for an Indefinite Period"

https://cburrell.wordpress.com/2008/09/26/chesterton-on-chesterton-on-chaucer/

Old Possum's Book of Practical Cats by T. S. Eliot—This book has been adapted into various forms, including a musical called *Cats* by Andrew Lloyd Webber.

Audio

Pygmalion relies on correct pronunciation for some of its humor, so it is best to listen to a professional audio recording.

Unabridged audiobook: http://amzn.to/2sUrmvu

An amateur performance of *Pygmalion* is available at:

http://librivox.org/pygmalion-by-george-bernard-shaw/

Music

"Shaw And The Don: George Bernard Shaw's Reception Of Mozart's Don Giovanni": Be sure to read this interesting article about Mozart's influence on Shaw's writings.

https://excellence-in-literature.com/
bernard-shaws-reception-of-mozarts-don-giovanni

Listen to some clips from the 1956 soundtrack of *My Fair Lady*. Notice how musical style creates a mood or atmosphere that heightens the drama of each plot twist.

http://amzn.to/2sf77Xo

Video

When you study a drama, you must see it performed in order to fully understand it. It is helpful to see both versions listed below:

Pygmalion (1938) with Wendy Hiller and Leslie Howard

https://excellence-in-literature.com/pygmalion-the-1938-movie/

My Fair Lady (1964) with Audrey Hepburn and Rex Harrison (recommended)

https://excellence-in-literature.com/my-fair-lady-1964-movie-trailer/

http://amzn.to/2tdvV6U

Watch an interesting video clip of George Bernard Shaw paying tribute to Albert Einstein in 1930:

http://nobelprize.org/nobel_prizes/literature/laureates/1925/shaw-docu.htm

This excellent resource offers background notes on the transformation of the Pygmalion story into the film *My Fair Lady*, as well as a few brief clips from the film:

http://www.reelclassics.com/Musicals/Fairlady/fairlady.htm

Visual Arts

Brown University Library offers a look at some of George Bernard Shaw's first editions and sketches, including *Everybody's Magazine*, November, 1914 and the first American publication of *Pygmalion*.

http://library.brown.edu/exhibits/archive/shaw/plays.html

View over 150 photos from *My Fair Lady* with Audrey Hepburn.

http://www.imdb.com/title/tt0058385/mediaindex

Here's a photo and article about the odd little rotating hut where George Bernard Shaw wrote:

http://honestarchitecture.blogspot.com/2010/05/george-bernard-shaw-and-marvelous.html

George Bernard Shaw's home in England:

http://flickr.com/photos/ishida/2468290477/in/pool-nationaltrust

Assignment Schedule

Week 1

Read Bulfinch's version of the legend of Pygmalion and Galatea.

http://flickr.com/photos/ishida/2468290477/in/pool-nationaltrust

Rewrite the legend (at least 300 words) with a contemporary setting and characters. What if a modern Pygmalion created Galatea as a computer graphic? Or papier-mâché? Refer to the creative writing section of your writer's handbook if you have difficulty imagining a different version of the story.

Be sure to refer to your writer's handbook if you have questions about grammar, structure, or style.

Week 2

Read *Pygmalion* and begin working through the context resources. Follow the model in the "Formats and Models" chapter to write an Author Profile.

Week 3

Complete context resources, and watch *Pygmalion* and/or *My Fair Lady* if possible. Begin drafting a 500-word essay on the topic below. I recommend that you follow the writing process outlined in the "How to Write an Essay" chapter, consulting the models in the Formats and Models chapter and your writer's handbook as needed.

Model: Literary Analysis Essay and MLA Format Model

Prompt: Eliza's character changes through the course of the play, both externally and internally. Trace the changes, particularly internal, and consider which is most important to the story. Discuss Eliza's transformation, and consider whether Higgins also experiences change, and how their change or lack of change affects the story.

Turn in the draft at the end of the week, so your writing mentor can evaluate it using the Content standards (Ideas/Concepts and Organization) on the rubric.

Week 4

Use the feedback on the rubric along with the writing mentor's comments to revise your paper. Before turning in the final draft, be sure you have addressed any issues marked on the evaluation rubric, and verify that the thesis is clear and your essay is well-organized. Use your writer's handbook to check grammar or punctuation so that your essay will be free from mechanical errors. Turn in the essay at the end of the week so that the writing mentor can use the evaluation rubric in the "How to Evaluate" chapter to check your work.

Module 1.6

Treasure Island by Robert Louis Stevenson(1850–1894)

*"Quiet minds cannot be perplexed or frightened but go on in fortune or misfortune
at their own private pace, like a clock during a thunderstorm."*

—Robert Louis Stevenson

Focus Text

Treasure Island by Robert Louis Stevenson

Honors Texts

Kidnapped by Robert Louis Stevenson

Literary Period

Romantic

Module Focus

You will begin to recognize the characteristics of the classic quest tale.

Introduction

In this 1883 romance (be sure to look at the definition of "romance" in the glossary), Robert Louis Stevenson presents a rollicking tale of young Jim Hawkins and his quest for buried treasure. Stevenson deftly sketches memorable characters, including the menacing Long John Silver whose name is known by many who have never read *Treasure Island*.

Something to think about . . .

The quest is one of the most ancient and beloved plots. Early examples of this story form include Homer's *Odyssey*, the Arthurian legend's quest for the Holy Grail, fairy tales in which a knight rescues a fair maiden from a dragon or other menace, and many more adventures.

One of the most famous modern examples of a quest tale is Frodo's quest in *The Lord of the Rings*. Think of other quest tales that you have read, and look for similarities in the elements of plot, theme, characterization, setting, and style. Which elements are most similar, and which are most different?

Be sure to notice . . .

Jim is transformed from a naïve boy to an intelligent and resourceful young man. Can you identify catalysts for each stage of the transformation? Also notice the symbolism in the use of the color black.

Context Resources

You will find a clickable list of the links in this chapter on the EIL website:

https://excellence-in-literature.com/curriculum-user-content/e1-context-resources/ eil-1-6-stevenson-context/

Readings

A free PDF volume of *The Letters of Robert Louis Stevenson: Volume One* can be downloaded from the link below. This collection begins with charming childhood missives to his parents, and continues with a fascinating array of letters to friends and family. If you like Stevenson, I think you will enjoy these.

https://en.wikisource.org/wiki/The_Letters_of_Robert_Louis_Stevenson_Volume_1

If you would like to read more of Stevenson's writings, here is a collection of many of his works in PDF format. Enjoy!

http://robert-louis-stevenson.org/rlsworks/

It is interesting to read "The Gold Bug," a story by Edgar Allen Poe that influenced Stevenson as he was writing *Treasure Island*.

https://excellence-in-literature.com/the-gold-bug-by-edgar-allan-poe/

Here is a link to G. K. Chesterton's brief essay about Stevenson. Do not miss it!

https://excellence-in-literature.com/stevenson-by-g-k-chesterton

The Author's Life

Stevenson's life was as interesting as the characters he created—I think you will enjoy reading about him.

The Treasure Hunter: The Story of Robert Louis Stevenson by Isabel Proudfit, Illustrated by Hardie Bramatky. New York: Julian Messner, Inc., 1940. (Alternate resource: Robert Louis Stevenson by Margaret Moyes Black or other brief biography.)

Robert Louis Stevenson by G. K. Chesterton (1902. London : Hodder & Stoughton.) This book contains many photographs and is distinct from the 1927 critical study by GKC with the same title.

The Life of Robert Louis Stevenson for Boys and Girls, by Jacqueline M. Overton- Despite its unfortunate name, this is a decent short illustrated biography. You may find it at your local library, or as an e-book at the following link:

http://www.gutenberg.org/etext/15547

Robert Louis Stevenson: A Record, An Estimate, and A Memorial by Alexander Hay Japp. This 1905 biography is available through Amazon, or as a free e-book:

http://www.gutenberg.org/etext/590

Brandeis University provides another interesting biography, as well as background information about the writing of *Treasure Island* and other works by Stevenson:

http://people.brandeis.edu/~teuber/stevensonbio.html

Poetry

Stevenson wrote many poems, including the well-known *A Child's Garden of Verses*. His other poetry collections included *Songs of Travel* and *Underwoods*. Read whichever collection you can find at your local library, or at this page:

http://www.poetryloverspage.com/poets/stevenson/stevenson_ind.html

The Academy of American Poets offers "A Brief Guide to Romanticism."

http://www.poets.org/viewmedia.php/prmMID/5670

Audio

You will enjoy Jim Hodges' outstanding recorded version of *Treasure Island.*

http://jimhodgesaudiobooks.com/classic_literature-treasure_island.php

Old Time Radio offers Mercury Theatre's *Treasure Island,* an abridged production (not a substitute for the entire book; just an optional and entertaining supplement.

https://archive.org/details/OTRCFR-TreasureIsand

Music

Did you know that Robert Louis Stevenson was a composer as well as an author? He studied music, and was an amateur composer of light, salon-type music, typical of California in the 1880s. J. F. M. Russell has put together an excellent site about Stevenson's musical talents, along with a collection of his compositions:

https://sites.google.com/a/music-of-robert-louis-stevenson.org/introduction/home

Richard Dury's site contains a list of musical settings of Stevenson's poems; derivative works, including operas, musicals, and songs; instrumental music; and music that Stevenson wrote:

http://www.robert-louis-stevenson.org/richard-dury-archive/music.htm

Video

Treasure Island has been filmed many times—look for the 1934 or 1950 version at your local library. This website lists all of the film versions of *Treasure Island*:

http://www.robert-louis-stevenson.org/richard-dury-archive/films-rls-treasure-island.html

Visual Arts

NOTE: You may use a college art history book or an art book for younger students, such as *The Annotated Mona Lisa.* to study art from Stevenson's era.

American realist artist N. C. Wyeth illustrated the 1911 edition of *Treasure Island.* Although he illustrated over 100 other books, this was considered his masterpiece, and with income from it, he was able to pay for his studio.

http://brandywine.doetech.net/results.cfm?ParentID=81987#

Additional Reading

The University of South Carolina has created an excellent online exhibition on Stevenson and his works. Be sure to read through all the "Islands" here:

http://www.sc.edu/library/spcoll/britlit/rls/rls.html

The Robert Louis Stevenson Website offers insight into Stevenson as "a poet, a playwright, a Gothicist, a historian, an anthropologist, a Victorian, and a Postmodernist."

http://www.robert-louis-stevenson.org/

Places to Go

You may visit Silverado Museum, dedicated to all things Stevenson, in St. Helena, California.

http://www.silveradomuseum.org

Another interesting site to visit would be the home in Samoa where Stevenson lived the last five years of his life. It is now the Robert Louis Stevenson Museum at Vailima, Western Samoa.

http://www.robert-louis-stevenson.org/museums/109-samoa-museum-western-samoa

Assignment Schedule

Week 1

Begin reading the context resources and the novel, and follow the model in the Formats and Models chapter to write an Author Profile. Be sure to refer to your writer's handbook if you have questions about grammar, structure, or style.

Week 2

Finish context readings, continue *Treasure Island*.

When you finish the novel, write a historical approach paper on the period from approximately 1650-1725 that is sometimes referred to as the "Golden Age of Piracy." You will find the format and a sample paper in the "Formats and Models" chapter. In addition to the context links I have provided, you may use other resources such as your encyclopedia, the library, and quality Internet resources to complete this assignment.

Week 3

Begin drafting a 500-word paper on one of the topics below. I recommend that you follow the writing process outlined in the "How to Write an Essay" chapter, consulting the models in the Formats and Models chapter and your writer's handbook as needed.

Model: Literary Analysis Essay and MLA Format Model

Prompt: Identify two codes of conduct referred to in the story, and their basis (possibly including scripture, chivalry, honor among thieves, and so forth). What social and cultural factors might cause different characters to adopt or abandon a particular code of conduct, and what might be the consequences for breaking with an accepted code? Use specific quotes and examples from the text to illustrate your points.. Be sure to provide specific textual support for your thesis.

Turn in the draft at the end of the week, so your writing mentor can evaluate it using the Content standards (Ideas/Concepts and Organization) on the rubric.

Week 4

Use the feedback on the rubric along with the writing mentor's comments to revise your paper. Before turning in the final draft, be sure you have addressed any issues marked on the evaluation rubric, and verify that the thesis is clear and your essay is well-organized. Use your writer's handbook to check grammar or punctuation so that your essay will be free from mechanical errors. Turn in the essay at the end of the week so that the writing mentor can use the evaluation rubric in the "How to Evaluate" chapter to check your work.

Module 1.7

Animal Farm by George Orwell (1903–1950)

*Animal Farm was the first book in which I tried, with full consciousness of what I was doing,
to fuse political purpose and artistic purpose into one whole..*

—George Orwell

Focus Text

Animal Farm by George Orwell

Honors Texts

1984 by George Orwell and

Fahrenheit 451 by Ray Bradbury

Literary Period

Realist

Module Focus

This module offers an introduction to political satire in a grown-up version of the beast fable.

Introduction

Animal Farm is an allegorical satire in the form of a beast fable. Although it is a story about animals, there is no danger that it might be mistaken for a children's book. This little novel was a political hot potato when it was written in 1944, and

George Orwell's regular publisher declined to publish it. Orwell even wrote a special preface for one edition, complaining about unofficial British censorship of the book, stating that *Animal Farm* was censored, "not because the Government intervened but because of a general tacit agreement that 'it wouldn't do' to mention that particular fact" (anti-Lenin sentiment). Ironically, this preface does not appear in many editions.

In the Ukraine, a special edition of *Animal Farm* was printed and handed out to displaced Soviet citizens after WWII. Because these copies were printed on illegal presses as propaganda, they were confiscated by American occupation forces and handed over to the Soviet government. Despite these difficulties, *Animal Farm* is included on many "great books" lists because it is hauntingly effective both as a story and as a vehicle for political commentary.

Something to think about . . .

The written word can have a powerful impact on people and on governments. Do you think the impact of *Animal Farm* is increased or decreased by its allegorical form? Why do you think Orwell chose a beast fable to convey his political points?

Be sure to notice . . .

George Orwell chose not to write under his own name. What was his real name, and why did he write under a pseudonym?

Context Resources

You will find a clickable list of the links in this chapter on the EIL website:

> https://excellence-in-literature.com/curriculum-user-content/e1-context-resources/eil-1-7-orwell-context/

Readings

In "Politics and the English Language" (1946), George Orwell reveals many of the ideas that are important to him, along with some excellent advice for writers. What are the six rules Orwell prescribes for writers?

http://www.orwell.ru/library/essays/politics/english/e_polit/

Orwell's essay, "Why I Write," from which the quote at the beginning of the module was excerpted, includes some very interesting insights into his early life as part of the background for why he has chosen to be a writer. What are the four motivations he writes about? What can you determine about his worldview?

http://orwell.ru/library/essays/wiw/english/e_wiw

Be sure to read this warm and spirited essay by Orwell, written in defense of fellow British writer, P. G. Wodehouse. If you are not familiar with the hilarious Wodehouse, the essay will serve as an introduction, but more importantly, it will give you a look at Orwell's character and values, and the political climate and issues that were important while he was writing.

http://theorwellprize.co.uk/george-orwell/by-orwell/essays-and-other-works/in-defence-of-p-g-wodehouse/

After you read Orwell's defense of Wodehouse, you will probably enjoy a sample of Wodehouse humor. He is most famous for his Bertie and Jeeves stories, but he also wrote many short stories. Here is his version of a King Arthur tale:

https://excellence-in-literature.com/sir-agravaine-by-p-g-wodehouse

You can read *Animal Farm* as an online book:

http://gutenberg.net.au/ebooks01/0100011h.html

The Author's Life

George Orwell: A Life in Pictures is a well-done BBC documentary on Orwell's life:

https://excellence-in-literature.com/george-orwell-a-life-in-pictures-a-documentary

George Orwell: Battling Big Brother by Tanya Agathocleous (2000) is a good, brief biography that will give you an overview of Orwell's life and the events that shaped his thoughts.

Timeline of George Orwell's life:

https://excellence-in-literature.com/george-orwell-timeline-by-steven-kreis/

There is a short, introductory biography at:

https://www.britannica.com/biography/George-Orwell

Another, longer biography is available at the Oxford Dictionary of National Biography:

http://www.oxforddnb.com/public/dnb/31915.html

The BBC has an online archive of letters from George Orwell, dating from the years he worked for the network as a Talks Producer.

http://www.bbc.co.uk/archive/orwell/

Poetry

Orwell occasionally wrote poetry, and one of his first efforts was published when he was 11 years old.

https://excellence-in-literature.com/george-orwell-resources/

One rather odd example of Orwell's poetry, supposedly inspired by a toothpaste advertisement, can be read here:

http://www.bbc.co.uk/archive/orwell/

Be sure to read Orwell's interesting and thought-provoking essay on "Poetry and the Microphone." In it, you will read very clear instructions for how to share poetry with those who are not accustomed to it. You will also see more evidence of Orwell's worldview.

http://www.george-orwell.org/Poetry_and_the_Microphone/0.html

Audio

If you would like to listen to an audiobook of *Animal Farm*, you may find it at your local library, or obtain it online.

http://amzn.to/2sN6R5A

This NPR report marking the 60th anniversary of *Animal Farm* is an excellent introduction to the book and its ideas. To hear the original audio, click on "Listen" or the sound symbol (just under the title).

http://www.npr.org/templates/story/story.php?storyId=4803830

Music

This site contains the complete written lyrics of all the songs in *Animal Farm*.

http://www.phil.muni.cz/angl/gw/farmww.html

Animal Farm has been produced as a puppet musical. You may click on the link below to view a PDF performance guide with photos and information about the production, as well as ideas for activities to do on your own.

https://www.dramaticpublishing.com/animal-farm

Video

You may visit the website of the puppet musical of *Animal Farm*, which has still photos of the production, as well as an educator's study guide.

https://web.archive.org/web/20050909193616/http://www.synapseproductions.org/whatson/afinfo.html

An animated version of *Animal Farm* was financed by the Central Intelligence Agency of the United States (CIA) and made in 1954.

https://excellence-in-literature.com/animal-farm-by-george-orwell-the-1954-movie/

A live-action film was made for Hallmark Films in 1999. You may be able to find this at your local library. I recommend reading the book before you watch the film. You may watch the film trailer at the link below:

http://us.imdb.com/title/tt0204824/

You may learn more about Russian culture through classics such as *Dr. Zhivago*, *Anna Karenina*, and *War and Peace*, but themes can be very dark, so these are optional.

Visual Arts

View photos of Orwell, his works, and the places that influenced his writing.

http://orwell.ru/bio/gallery/english/

More photos of George Orwell's London and gravesite can be found here:

https://suttoncourtenay.co.uk/village-information/george-orwell-grave/

Historical Context

Read this overview of Russian history. Pay particular attention to the sections entitled "The Path to Revolution" and "The Soviet Era":

http://www.geographia.com/russia/rushis01.htm

In your encyclopedia, read entries about communism, socialism, and totalitarianism.

Here are resources that draw comparisons between the characters in *Animal Farm* to Russian Revolution figures and events.

https://excellence-in-literature.com/animal-farm-and-its-relationship-to-history

This comprehensive, well-researched Canadian site contains excellent information and links to Orwell resources, including full-length works, photographs, essays and news articles.

https://web-beta.archive.org/web/20110321044838/http://www.netcharles.com:80/orwell/

You will find more detailed information about the characters in *Animal Farm* at this site:

https://web-beta.archive.org/web/20110927022153/http://www.netcharles.com/orwell/articles/col-afcp.htm

If you enjoy taking quizzes, you will find a 20-question online quiz at Online Literature. (This site supports itself through advertising, so be sure your browser's pop-up blocker is activated before visiting).

http://www.online-literature.com/quiz.php?quizid=200

Eyewitness: Russia by Kathleen Berton Murrell is the place to start for a look at the historical context of this module. Look for it at your library or bookstore.

PBS offers "The Face of Russia," an online introduction to Russian history. Look at the timeline section, and click over to the part that covers the 20th century. You can click on images for more information about people and events.

http://www.pbs.org/weta/faceofrussia/intro.html

The Library of Congress offers an online text about Russia and its history and culture.

https://www.loc.gov/collections/country-studies/?q=russia

Here is a brief video history of Russia illustrated by birds-eye view maps, so that you can see the size of the country. Remember, YouTube is not a scholarly source, but little videos like this can be a starting point for further research.

https://excellence-in-literature.com/russian-history/

Literary Context

Aesop's Fables: These are some of the best-known examples of beast fables. Read or listen to a few, and compare them with *Animal Farm* in form and purpose.

http://aesopfables.com/

A Modest Proposal by Jonathan Swift is a very funny example of political satire from 1729.

https://excellence-in-literature.com/a-modest-proposal-by-jonathan-swift

"Politics and the English Language" is Orwell's excellent 1946 article on writing. Do not miss it!

http://www.orwell.ru/library/essays/politics/english/e_polit/

Quotes

The George Orwell website has most of Orwell's works, including a nice selection of quotes. Copy at least two of them in your notebook.

http://www.george-orwell.org/l_quotes.html

Places to Go

If you are fortunate enough to be in London, you may take a walking tour of sites related to George Orwell

http://orwellslondontour.webs.com/

George Orwell's birthplace in Bihar, India, is being turned into a museum.

https://www.theguardian.com/world/2014/jun/30/george-orwell-birthplace-motihari-bihar-india-museum

Assignment Schedule

Week 1

Read the context readings. In this module, it is important to read the context materials first, so you will better understand the focus text.

Begin reading the context resources. Follow the model in the Formats and Models chapter to write a brief Author Profile. Be sure to refer to your writer's handbook if you have questions about grammar, structure, or style.

Week 2

Read the focus text. It is a very short book, but it contains some very deep ideas. As you read, you may want to make a list of the characters in the back of the book, and link them to the real-life figures that Orwell intended them to represent.

Write a Historical Period/Event Approach Paper on the Russian Revolution, following the format in the Formats and Models chapter. In addition to the context links I have provided, you may use other resources such as your encyclopedia, the library, and quality Internet resources to complete this assignment.

Week 3

Begin drafting a 600-word paper on one of the topics below. I recommend that you follow the writing process outlined in the "How to Write an Essay" chapter, consulting the models in the Formats and Models chapter and your writer's handbook as needed.

1- Model: Literary Analysis Essay and MLA Format Model

Prompt: Orwell explores the use of rhetoric in *Animal Farm*. Notice how the character of Squealer uses language as an instrument of social control, and how the pigs rewrite history. Discuss how and why the use of rhetoric is central to the novel. Support your thesis with appropriate examples from the text.

2- Model: *Animal Farm* and MLA Format Model

Prompt: Choose a political event and write a beast fable about it in the style of George Orwell's *Animal Farm*. You may make it as long as it needs to be in order to clearly tell your story.

Turn in the draft at the end of the week, so your writing mentor can evaluate it using the Content standards (Ideas/Concepts and Organization) on the rubric.

Week 4

Use the feedback on the rubric, along with the writing mentor's comments, to revise your paper. Before turning in the final draft, be sure you have addressed any issues marked on the evaluation rubric, and verify that the thesis is clear and your essay is well-organized. Use your writer's handbook to check grammar or punctuation so that your essay will be free from mechanical errors. Turn in the essay at the end of the week so that the writing mentor can use the evaluation rubric in the "How to Evaluate" chapter to check your work.

Module 1.8

The Tempest by William Shakespeare (1564-1616)

What's past is prologue.

—The Tempest, 2.1

Focus Text

The Tempest by William Shakespeare

Honors Texts

A Midsummer Night's Dream by William Shakespeare

Literary Period

Renaissance

Module Focus

You will learn the literary concepts of romance and comedy, and become acquainted with Shakespeare's distinctive methods of characterization.

Introduction

The Tempest, a romance that is usually classified with Shakespeare's comedy plays, is a delightful introduction to Shakespeare's vivid characters. Although the entire action of the play takes place in less than a day, most of the characters experience a dramatic transformation in status, role, personality, or appearance, or some combination of these. Even the plot undergoes a transformation, preventing the play from becoming one of Shakespeare's tragedies.

You will notice that there are many mentions of noise, sound, or music in the play. Be sure to observe how the sound theme moves the plot forward, and how the choice of noises affects the mood of the play. There is one speech I would like for you notice in particular, in Act III, Scene ii, in which Caliban speaks of the noises of the island. Shakespeare uses this speech, and Caliban's description of what he hears, to transform, or at least add to, the reader's perspective about the character of Caliban. This is one of the techniques that makes Shakespeare a master of his craft.

Another device to notice is the "play within a play." This is another dramatic effect that Shakespeare uses to add additional layers of context to the plot. In *The Tempest*, you will see this in the masque, presented in the fourth act of the play. A masque, short for "masquerade," is a type of dramatic performance, that was often performed in 16th and 17th century England and Europe as an elaborate royal entertainment, consisting of pantomime, dancing, dialogue, and song. What do you think was the purpose of the masque in *The Tempest*? What does it contribute to your understanding of the elements of plot, theme, setting, characters, and style?

Something to think about . . .

The traditional five-act play form that was especially popular during the Elizabethan era seems perfect for *The Tempest*. As you listen to the play, you will notice the sequence of exposition, rising action (sometimes known as "complication"), climax, falling action, and resolution (sometimes called "catastrophe"), with each portion of the sequence contained neatly within an act of the play.

How might the use of this standard form (almost a template) have helped Shakespeare compose and write quickly? More interestingly, how could a carefully defined form help you write a well-organized story or essay for any assignment?

Be sure to notice . . .

This play is set on an island, and seems to have been inspired by some of the exploration of Shakespeare's day, particularly a 1609 voyage to Virginia in which one vessel of the nine that had sailed was shipwrecked in the Bermudas. Although the ship was thought to be permanently lost, it arrived in Jamestown the following spring.

Context Resources

You will find a clickable list of the links in this chapter on the EIL website:

https://excellence-in-literature.com/curriculum-user-content/e1-context-resources/
eil-1-8-shakespeare-context/

Readings

Shakespeare by Peter Chrisp: This Dorling Kindersley Eyewitness book is a valuable, inexpensive introduction to the world of Shakespeare, and includes a splendid synopsis of each of his plays.

This delightful introduction to Shakespeare's Grammar will help you understand his writings much more easily.

http://www.bardweb.net/grammar/grammar.html

Absolute Shakespeare offers an excellent introduction to *The Tempest*, including character lists and a synopsis.

http://www.absoluteshakespeare.com/guides/tempest/tempest.htm

Charles and Mary Lamb rewrote all of Shakespeare's plays for children. You will probably find their *Tales from Shakespeare* at your local library, or you can read it online. Here is a link to their short version of *The Tempest*:

https://excellence-in-literature.com/
the-tempest-tales-from-shakespeare-by-charles-and-mary-lamb/

Life in Elizabethan England: These sites offer links so that you can explore interesting context details of Elizabethan England, including fashion, household management, heraldry, education, occupations, and more.

http://elizabethan.org/compendium/

http://www.britainexpress.com/History/Elizabethan_life.htm

An excerpt from *Foxe's Book of Martyrs*: The 16th century was a time of religious conflict in England, and executions were common. Read the sad story of the execution of 17-year-old Lady Jane Grey at the link below.

http://excellence-in-literature.com/excellence-in-lit/british-lit/e4-resources/
execution-of-lady-jane-grey-from-foxes-book-of-martyrs

Learn about the 16th-Century zeitgeist (spirit of the age): At the scholarly Norton site, you can read about the literary world of the 16th century, and how it affected Shakespeare's writing.

http://wwnorton.com/college/english/nael/16century/welcome.htm

Shakespeare's Food Poesies: Food shows up in many places in Shakespeare's dramas, and on this site there is an alphabetically organized encyclopedia of quotes. It is an interesting way to see what was in the Elizabethan diet.

https://archive.is/E099b

The Author's Life

Invitation to the Classics edited by Cowan and Guinness: If you own or can borrow this book, read the chapter on Shakespeare and the sections on Western Social and Political Philosophy (190) and German Classics (215). The editors approach their topic from a Christian worldview, which may be helpful for you.

The Shakespeare Resource Center provides a good introductory biography of Shakespeare, as well as many other useful resources.

http://www.bardweb.net/man.html

Timeline of important events in Shakespeare's life:

http://absoluteshakespeare.com/trivia/timeline/timeline.htm

The Seven Ages of Shakespeare's Life

http://ise.uvic.ca/Library/SLT/life/lifesubj.html

Who wrote Shakespeare's works? Now that you've read about Shakespeare, you should know that there is an ongoing controversy about who actually wrote all his works. The Shakespeare Oxford site offers "A Beginner's Guide to the Shakespeare Authorship Problem." Do not miss this!

http://www.shakespeare-oxford.com/?p=35

Poetry

All of Shakespeare's poetry (and plays) can be found in a well-organized, searchable database at:

http://www.opensourceshakespeare.org/

Visit this page to read poetry from Shakespeare's contemporaries, including Queen Elizabeth, Sir Philip Sydney, and Sir Walter Raleigh.

https://excellence-in-literature.com/poetry-by-shakespeare-contemporaries

Other poets, such as W. H. Auden, have composed poetry based on characters from *The Tempest*. You may read one example by Robert Browning, "Caliban upon Setebos" at:

https://excellence-in-literature.com/caliban-upon-setebos-by-robert-browning

Audio

The Tempest as a professional-recorded audio:

http://amzn.to/2rps7oS

The entire play is available for listening and reading along from *Speak the Speech: Universal Shakespeare Broadcasting*. Be sure to read the Synopsis and Director's Notes before listening. Unlike the speedy dialog heard in many Shakespeare readings, the actors speak at a comfortable pace for following along.

http://www.speak-the-speech.org/thetempestpage.htm

Music

Tchaikovsky wrote a Symphonic Overture based on *The Tempest*. You may listen to a sample of each movement at Classical Archives, or you may also download it for $0.99/track.

https://excellence-in-literature.com/tempest-overture-tchaikovsky

The Folger Shakespeare created a collection of Songs and Dances from *The Tempest*, and you may listen to Caliban's song and "Where the Bee Sucks," beautifully sung and accompanied by appropriate instruments such as the lute and viol at this site:

http://www.shakespeareinamericanlife.org/stage/music/tempest/index.cfm

Jean Sibelius composed orchestral music for the play in 1926. You may see the complete list of songs, and hear samples at:

http://www.emusic.com/album/Jean-Sibelius-SIBELIUS-The-Tempest-MP3-Download/10898001.html

Music of the Renaissance: This website offers free midi-files of Renaissance music, organized by composer. You can listen to the sort of music Shakespeare might have heard.

http://www.curtisclark.org/emusic/renaissa.html

For an entirely different sound, you may want to check your library for a copy of Duke Ellington's jazz album, *Such Sweet Thunder,* composed after Ellington played at the Shakespeare festival in Stratford, Ontario. The title is taken from *A Midsummer Night's Dream,* and the individual pieces are composed as expressions of individual characters. You may read a brief essay (be sure to click on "continue" at the bottom of each page) about the album at the Shakespeare in American Life site below. To learn more, click on the left-hand link to hear Duke Ellington's granddaughter Mercedes Ellington talk about the album.

http://www.shakespeareinamericanlife.org/stage/music/thunder/dukeellington.cfm

You may also listen to a brief NPR interview about *Such Sweet Thunder,* with clips of two pieces from the album. The interview mentions Ellington's goal of creating a mood that illustrates each of his chosen characters. The album provides an interesting contrast to the medieval music, and the interview may help you understand it a bit better.

http://www.npr.org/templates/story/story.php?storyId=4543727

Video

This is a play, so you need to watch it in order to fully understand it. Many libraries carry videos of Shakespeare's plays, or you can purchase it at Amazon.com:

http://amzn.to/2rpxrRX

A "60 Second Shakespeare" production of *The Tempest* can be seen at:

http://www.bbc.co.uk/drama/shakespeare/60secondshakespeare/watch/fearnhill_tempest.shtmll

Visual Arts

Take a virtual tour of the Globe Theatre in London.

http://www.shakespearesglobe.com/about-us/virtual-tour

Emory University has a collection of links to paintings of scenes and characters from *The Tempest*. Here are a few interesting images, most accompanied by appropriate lines from the play:

http://www.english.emory.edu/classes/Shakespeare_Illustrated/Miranda1.html - This lovely painting by John Waterhouse is my favorite image from this play.

http://www.english.emory.edu/classes/Shakespeare_Illustrated/Romney.Tempest.html

http://www.english.emory.edu/classes/Shakespeare_Illustrated/Goodall.Miranda.html

The Tate Museum in England has placed a large portion of its collection online in an easily searchable database. From the homepage, type "Caliban" in the search box, and you will see an interesting character sketch, assumed to be Caliban.

http://www.tate.org.uk/

Places to Go

The American Shakespeare Center in Staunton, Virginia offers performances in the Blackfriars Playhouse, a replica of William Shakespeare's original indoor theatre.

http://www.americanshakespearecenter.com/

The Folger Shakespeare Library, located on Capitol Hill in Washington, D. C., has a large collection of Shakespeare materials, including audio and video resources. Admission is free.

http://www.folger.edu/index.cfm

If you should happen to be in London, do not miss the Globe Theatre, which has been reconstructed to look much as it did in Shakespeare's day.

http://www.shakespeares-globe.org

Assignment Schedule

Week 1

Read the short version of *The Tempest* by Charles and Mary Lamb, and other context materials, especially the Eyewitness book and the readings about Shakespeare and Elizabethan England. Follow the model in the Formats and Models chapter to write an Author Profile. Be sure to refer to your writer's handbook if you have questions about grammar, structure, or style.

Week 2

Read the complete play, and listen to the play at Speak the Speech (in Audio Resources, above). Watch a video of the play.

Write a brief summary (about three sentences each) of each of the five acts of the play, using careful sentence structure and vivid, varied vocabulary. In addition to the context links in this module, you may use other resources such as your encyclopedia, the library, and quality Internet resources to complete this assignment.

Week 3

Begin drafting a 600-word paper on one of the topics below. I recommend that you follow the writing process outlined in the "How to Write an Essay" chapter, consulting the models in the Formats and Models chapter and your writer's handbook as needed.

1- Model: Literary Analysis Essay and MLA Format Model

Prompt: Shakespeare seemed to be concerned about addressing questions of justice in this play. Take particular note of the relationship between Prospero and Caliban, and Prospero and Ariel. How do these relationships change over the course of the story, and how does this fit with the identification of *The Tempest* as a romance or comedy? Be sure to use quotations from the play as support for your viewpoint.

2- Model: MLA Format Model

Prompt: You are a news reporter on a neighboring island. You have noticed some unusual activity on Prospero's island, and you travel over to investigate. "Interview" two or more characters, and write a news story, using the language of the day (similar to King James-style English) about the shipwreck and subsequent events, using a few quotes from your interview subjects. Be sure to use proper journalistic format and Elizabethan vocabulary.

If you need help with journalistic format, here are some good tips:

https://excellence-in-literature.com/journalism-story-structure-by-mark-grabowski/

Turn in the draft at the end of the week, so your writing mentor can evaluate it using the Content standards (Ideas/Concepts and Organization) on the rubric.

Week 4

Use the feedback on the rubric, along with the writing mentor's comments, to revise your paper. Before turning in the final draft, be sure you have addressed any issues marked on the evaluation rubric, and verify that the thesis is clear and your essay is well-organized. Use your writer's handbook to check grammar or punctuation so that your essay will be free from mechanical errors. Turn in the essay at the end of the week so that the writing mentor can use the evaluation rubric in the "How to Evaluate" chapter to check your work.

Module 1.9

Gulliver's Travels by Jonathan Swift (1667-1745)

Satire is a sort of glass wherein beholders do generally discover everybody's face but their own; which is the chief reason for that kind reception it meets with in the world, and that so very few are offended with it.

—Jonathan Swift

Focus Text

Gulliver's Travels by Jonathan Swift (1726)

Honors Text

The Pilgrim's Progress by John Bunyan (1678)

Just a few years before Swift wrote *Gulliver's Travels*, John Bunyan wrote a very different sort of travel narrative. Read or listen to his allegory, using the links from this page listed below. Compare *Pilgrim's Progress* with *Gulliver's Travels*, and note the contrasts between the style and focus of each book.

http://www.ccel.org/ccel/bunyan/pilgrim.html

Literary Period

Neoclassical

Module Focus

Jonathan Swift's use of satire is an attack on Enlightenment (Age of Reason) ideas. Students will become acquainted with Swift and his masterpiece, *Gulliver's Travels*, and with the ideas of the Enlightenment and the use of satire.

Introduction

Like many modern humorists, Jonathan Swift was a controversial figure. He was an Anglo-Irish clergyman who used satire to point out the follies and illogical thinking of politicians, scientists, scholars, and his contemporaries. In doing so, he managed to offend almost everyone at one time or another. His sharp observations pointed out the folly of arrogance, and they highlighted the weaknesses of the Enlightenment's abandonment of common sense and experience in favor of an unfettered belief in abstract reasoning and the perfectibility of mankind.

Something to think about . . .

Although this novel has sometimes been mistaken for a children's story, it is actually a bitingly satirical social commentary. Swift was deeply concerned that people repeatedly choose to act irrationally, despite the promptings of judgment and common sense. His view of human nature as fundamentally flawed seems theologically based, though his personal beliefs have been questioned and often misunderstood as misanthropy.

Swift wrote *Gulliver's Travels* as part of a project by his authors' group, in which each writer would contribute a portion of the biography of a fictional character, Martinus Scriblerus. The project was conceived as a satirical look at modern man and his follies, and each author had something specific to satirize. Swift chose to use the format of "armchair travel" books that were popular at the time, satirizing the form itself, as well as the tendency of many readers to believe everything they read.

Be sure to notice . . .

The actual title of this book is *Travels Into Several Remote Nations of the World by Lemuel Gulliver*. Why do you think that Swift chose to write this in journal form? Does it make the events more or less plausible?

Gulliver's name contains the 16th-century root word "gull" (to fool or deceive) which is also found in the word "gullible" (easy to fool). As you read, consider what Swift might be implying with the choice of this name.

Context Resources

You will find a clickable list of the links in this chapter on the EIL website:

https://excellence-in-literature.com/curriculum-user-content/e1-context-resources/
eil-1-9-swift-context/

Readings

If possible, read the chapter on Jonathan Swift and Gulliver's Travels in *Invitation to the Classics* (complete bibliographic information in the Resources section of this book). It provides a clear and interesting look at Swift's worldview and the Enlightenment world in which he lived.

The Enlightenment (the Age of Reason): A Washington State University professor has posted an excellent explanation of this philosophic movement:

https://brians.wsu.edu/2016/10/12/the-enlightenment/

The *All About History* website offers a look at the Enlightenment as contrasted with Christianity. This is a very helpful discussion of the role the Enlightenment played in the transition between medieval and modern thought.

http://www.allabouthistory.org/age-of-reason.htm

The Norton Anthology of English Literature offers a concise, well-written analysis of Swift as an author and as a person. I recommend looking for used copies of the Norton anthologies at used bookstores, remainder tables, or online, because they contain extremely reliable, high quality author introductions and their chronological format makes it easy to see the literary context of the works we will study throughout *Excellence in Literature*. The 18th-century page of their companion website may be found at:

http://www.wwnorton.com/college/english/nael/18century/welcome.htm

Use your encyclopedia to look up "Enlightenment" and "Age of Reason." Note the major beliefs and philosophers of this movement. If you do not have an enclyclopedia, you can read a brief introduction online (just make sure that your browser's pop-up blocker is activated before clicking on the link below):

http://www.britannica.com/EBchecked/topic/188441/Enlightenment

At the website listed below, be sure to study the timelines that link Swift and Gulliver with the literary, artistic, scientific, and political developments of their historic period. If you study the timelines closely, you can see parallels between the things that happen to Gulliver and things happening in Swift's world.

http://www.wildsidz.com/beth/index.php?screen=gulliver

The Battle of the Books by Jonathan Swift (or as he titled it, "A Full and True Account OF THE B A T T E L Fought last F R I D A Y, Between the Antient and the Modern BOOKS IN St. J A M E S's LIBRARY") is a humorous essay from which the quote at the beginning of this chapter was taken. It is reproduced at

http://andromeda.rutgers.edu/~jlynch/Texts/battle.html

Another funny satirical essay by Swift is "A Modest Proposal." You may read it at the first link or listen to it at the second link.

https://excellence-in-literature.com/a-modest-proposal-by-jonathan-swift

http://librivox.org/a-modest-proposal-by-jonathan-swift/

The Author's Life

There are many full length biographies of Jonathan Swift, and those written by Irvin Ehrenpreis and Richard Quintana are particularly recommended by the authors of *Invitation to the Classics*. I have not encountered any that I feel are indispensable, so you may choose any brief biography from your library, as long as it's written for the middle grades or above.

https://excellence-in-literature.com/jonathan-swift-biography

You will find a brief biographical introduction in any of the recommended editions of the text. The A.A. Knopf 1925 edition has an excellent introduction by H.L. Mencken. As mentioned earlier, I also recommend the chapter on Swift in *Invitation to the Classics*.

A short online biography of Jonathan Swift by Professor David Cody can be found at:

http://www.victorianweb.org/previctorian/swift/bio.html

Poetry

Swift wrote several good poems, but I particularly want you to read his very funny "Verses on the Death of Dr. Swift, D.S.P.D."

https://excellence-in-literature.com/verses-on-the-death-of-dr-swift-d-s-p-d

Here is an analytical essay that may help you understand the poem.

https://excellence-in-literature.com/
fortunate-misfortunes-an-analysis-of-verses-on-the-death-of-dr-swift

You may find other samples of his poetry listed at the site below; I suggest reading at least one of his other poems.

http://rpo.library.utoronto.ca/poets/swift-jonathan

Swift's friend, Alexander Pope, was a splendid poet and writer. You may read some of his works on this site compiled by members of the English department at the University of Toronto. Read "Solitude: An Ode" and any other works you choose. I especially like the "Essay on Criticism."

http://rpo.library.utoronto.ca/poets/pope-alexander

Audio

Gulliver's Travels is quite funny, and the humor is often best appreciated when you hear the story read aloud. You may find professionally-produced copies of the unabridged audio book at your local library or online.

http://amzn.to/2tp8XKh

LibriVox offers a free amateur recording of *Gulliver's Travels* (quality of narration varies).

http://librivox.org/gullivers-travels-by-jonathan-swift/

Another option is a computer-generated audio book that can be downloaded at:

http://www.gutenberg.org/etext/9272

Music

In 1728, two years after the publication of *Gulliver's Travels*, German composer Georg Philipp Telemann wrote the "Gulliver Suite," a five-movement musical suite for two violins. If you can find it at your library, listen to it, and see how the musical mood of each movement reflects the book-related titles of each movement. You can also listen to brief free samples of the music at:

https://excellence-in-literature.com/jonathan-swift-resources/

The 18th century was a high point in classical music. Composers such as Bach, Mozart, Handel, Schumann, and Tchaikovsky were hard at work, creating masterpieces that continue to bring enormous pleasure to listeners around the globe. If you do not have CDs of these composer's works, get them from the library or visit www.pandora.com, and search for "Wolfgang Amadeus Mozart Radio," which I have enjoyed as I worked on this module. You may also listen to MIDI files of 18th-century music from:

http://www.midiworld.com/classic.htm

As a contrast to Swift's satire, you may enjoy listening to MIDI file recordings of the hymns of Charles Wesley, who lived during the same era as Swift. Swift may not have heard Wesley's compositions, but he most likely heard music in a very similar style. You will find an extensive collection of Wesley lyrics at:

https://www.umcmission.org/Find-Resources/Global-Praise-/Charles-Wesley-Hymns

You may learn more about 18th-century composers, and see a few art images of the era at:

http://www.rslade.co.uk/

Rutgers University also offers a good selection of links to more information on 18th century music at:

http://andromeda.rutgers.edu/~jlynch/18th/music.html

Video

Gulliver's Travels was made into an animated feature in 1939. This is now in the public domain, so you can watch it free:

https://excellence-in-literature.com/gullivers-travels-the-1939-movie/

The video biography, *The Famous Authors: Jonathan Swift* (Kultur Video, 2007) may be available at your library. It is also online:

http://amzn.to/2qBmQUE

The term "armchair traveler" was used to describe people who traveled vicariously through the writings and photographs of others. Modern armchair travelers still travel vicariously through books, blogs, and photos, but in addition, there are also virtual 360° tours through which you can explore sites such as the Taj Mahal or Kew Gardens.

Here is a link to a site that features some of these tours. You will need to have Java installed on your computer in order to view them (you can download the program for free from http://www.java.com/en/).

http://www.armchair-travel.com/index.htm

Visual Arts

Illustrator Arthur Rackham created wonderful illustrations for *Gulliver's Travels*. You may view these at:

http://rackham.artpassions.net/gullivergallery.html

Swift lived and wrote during the Baroque period in art history. Major artists included Rembrandt van Rijn, Jan Vermeer, William Hogarth, Diego Velasquez, and Jean-Honoré Fragonard, among others. You may visit the Baroque section of the WebMuseum, Paris, at the site listed below (use Internet Explorer for best results). Click on the artists' names to see a brief biography and images of a few of their paintings. Each artist tells a story with his paintings, and by looking at a large number of them, you will soon be able to recognize the distinctive style and mood of the era. How does it relate or contrast to the style and mood of Swift's satire?

http://www.ibiblio.org/wm/paint/theme/baroque.html

You may read a brief overview of 18th-century art in your encyclopedia or at:

http://www.humanitiesweb.org/human.php?s=g&p=a&a=i&ID=464

Additional Resources

E-texts of Swift's works can be found at:

http://publicliterature.org/books/gullivers_travels/xaa.php

Some of the most notable quotes by Jonathan Swift can be found at the following links:

http://en.wikiquote.org/wiki/Jonathan_Swift

Two bits of trivia

1- I have never wanted a Yahoo e-mail address. After reading the book, do you?

2- It is said that Daniel Boone always carried a copy of *Gulliver's Travels* with him on his explorations. I wonder if he was inspired by Gulliver, or if he just found the book an entertaining diversion from his own journeys?

Places to Go

The Dublin Writers Museum features many Irish writers, including Jonathan Swift. In addition, Swift is honored with a monument in St Patrick's Cathedral and a bust in Trinity College Dublin's library.

http://www.writersmuseum.com/

Assignment Schedule

Week 1

Read and explore context materials, and begin reading *Gulliver's Travels*. Copy all the definitions of satire that you find, including the one at the beginning of this module (you should have at least three complete definitions). This will give you a better understanding of it than if you just read one or two. Follow the model in the Formats and Models chapter to write an Author Profile. Be sure to refer to your writer's handbook if you have questions about grammar, structure, or style.

Week 2

Continue with readings and write a Historical Period/Event Approach Paper on the European Enlightenment, which is also known as the Age of Reason, following the format in the Formats and Models chapter. In addition to the context links I have provided, you may use other resources such as your encyclopedia, the library, and quality Internet resources to complete this assignment.

Week 3

Begin drafting a 600-word paper on one of the topics below. I recommend that you follow the writing process outlined in the "How to Write an Essay" chapter, consulting the models in the Formats and Models chapter and your writer's handbook as needed.

1- Model: Literary Analysis Essay and MLA Format Model

Prompt: In his travel narrative, Swift seems to use size as a metaphor for morality. Discuss the correlation between size and morality in each of the societies that

Gulliver visits, and briefly consider other ways in which Swift seems to assess the relative moral state of those he visits.

2- MLA Format Model

Prompt: Write a travel journal for an imaginary trip to an imaginary country in the style of *Gulliver's Travels*. Your journal must contain at least three entries, and describe a world and a people that is different from any that Gulliver encountered. Make it long enough create a unified travel narrative, with a beginning, middle, and end.

Turn in the draft at the end of the week, so your writing mentor can evaluate it using the Content standards (Ideas/Concepts and Organization) on the rubric.

Week 4

Use the feedback on the rubric, along with the writing mentor's comments, to revise your paper. Before turning in the final draft, be sure you have addressed any issues marked on the evaluation rubric, and verify that the thesis is clear and your essay is well-organized. Use your writer's handbook to check grammar or punctuation so that your essay will be free from mechanical errors. Turn in the essay at the end of the week so that the writing mentor can use the evaluation rubric in the "How to Evaluate" chapter to check your work.

Honors

Excellence is doing ordinary things extraordinarily well.

—John W. Gardner

Key components of the Honors Option (in addition to regular assignments related to the focus text) include reading, writing, and a final exam. The reading is the most time-consuming element, as it is the foundation for both the writing assignment and the final exam. Be sure to create a schedule that makes it manageable:

- Extra reading with an approach paper for each book
- One 6- to 10-page research paper (depending on student's grade level)
- CLEP test for some levels

Extra Reading

Extra reading for honors students will be listed on the syllabus. Some items will be additional works by authors we are studying; other items will be context works that will help to round out knowledge of each literary period or understanding of the theme. Honors reading may be done during or between semesters and should be recorded in the reading log.

Approach Papers

For one full-length honors text per module, the student should complete an approach paper. If more than one honors text is suggested, the student may choose which to read (though it can be beneficial to read all of them) and which to use as the subject for the approach paper. It is not necessary to write more than one honors approach paper per module.

Research Paper

This 6- to 10-page paper, due two weeks after the end of the spring semester, will be a research paper on your choice of the authors you have studied this year. The paper will be presented in MLA format (http://owl.english.purdue.edu/owl/resource/747/01/) and will include a Works Cited page, with a minimum of four resources. Up to two of the resources may be Internet sources chosen in accordance with accepted academic standards. For detailed instructions on the process of researching, writing, and documenting a research paper, consult your writer's handbook.

Suggestions for the Author Research Paper

A research paper has been described as a thoughtful inquiry into a topic you find interesting. You will find detailed instructions in most writer's handbooks for how to do research, keep track of sources, list citations, format your research paper, and so forth. Once you have decided on the author who will be the focus of your Honors paper, here are things you may want to include:

- overview of the author's life
- people, groups, and events that influenced the author's life and writing
- overview of the author's body of work and his or her reputation among peers and in the general public
- analysis of one or more of the author's best- or least-known works
- how the author's work has influenced later writers or a genre of literature

CLEP Test

The comprehensive final exam, which can be taken at the end of the school year (or after next year study of *Literature and Composition*), will be the *Analyzing and Interpreting Literature* or *College Composition* CLEP. These 90-minute, multiple-choice, computer-based exams can be taken by appointment at a local college or community college. Many colleges and universities grant advanced placement and/or college credit (up to six credits) for a passing score on this exam, so it is well worth the effort. (I earned forty-five credits toward my B.A. by taking exams on subjects I had studied on my own.) You may learn more about CLEP exams at www.CollegeBoard.com.

Excellence in Literature: Assignment Checklist

Student: **School Year:**

Grade: **English I: Introduction to Literature**

	Week 1		Week 2		Week 3		Week 4	
	Assignment	Date	Assignment	Date	Assignment	Date	Assignment	Date
Module 1.1- Short Stories								
Module 1.2- Verne								
Module 1.3- Twain								
Module 1.4– Brontë								
Module 1.5- Shaw								
Module 1.6- Stevenson								
Module 1.7- Orwell								
Module 1.8- Shakespeare								
Module 1.9- Swift								
For each module, list the assignment and the date due or completed (your choice).								

Sample Listing

Module #- Example	Author profile	01/07	Approach paper	01/14	750-word essay draft	01/21	Final draft of essay	01/28

Excellence in Literature: Student Evaluation Summary

Student: **School Year:**

Letter Grade: **English I: Introduction to Literature**

	Ideas/ Concepts	Organi- zation	Voice	Word Choice	Sentence Fluency	Mechanics	Presen- tation	Total
Module 1.1- Short Stories								
Module 1.2- Verne								
Module 1.3- Twain								
Module 1.4- Brontë								
Module 1.5- Shaw								
Module 1.6- Stevenson								
Module 1.7- Orwell								
Module 1.8- Shakespeare								
Module 1.9- Swift								
Total								
Average								

Class Description

Introduction to Literature is a college-preparatory literature and composition course. Focus works, including novels, short stories, poems, and drama have been selected for literary quality and for their place in the historic development of literature.

Context readings provide background information about the author, and historic, literary, and artistic context of the focus work. Students will practice the skills of close literary analysis through essays, approach papers, and other writing.

Course Objectives

By the end of the course, students will:

- Understand the process of writing, including the use of tools such as a writer's handbook, dictionary, and thesaurus.
- Have specific understanding of selected representative texts by major authors of the periods studied.
- Have a general understanding of the historical and cultural contexts of the works.
- Be able to analyze literary texts and present thoughtfully developed ideas in writing.
- Demonstrate competence in essay organization, style, and mechanics.
- Demonstrate competence in the MLA style of source documentation.

Evaluations

Student writing is evaluated using the Excellence in Writing evaluation rubric. Each paper is analyzed and evaluated in the following seven areas: Ideas and Concepts, Organization, Voice, Word Choice, Sentence Fluency, Mechanics, and Presentation. Course grade is based upon essays (65%), shorter assignments (15%), vocabulary development (10%), and studentship (10%).

Comments

Formats and Models

Example is the school of mankind, and they will learn at no other.

—Edmund Burke

There is a long and honorable tradition of using models or samples to learn to write well. The formats and models are you find here will help you understand the elements of each kind of assignment you will do. Each basic type of paper practiced in EIL is presented with a "Format"—instructions for what each paper should contain—plus a "Model"—a student-written sample of what a completed paper might look like. These models have been used with the permission of some of my former students and are examples of what each type of assignment should contain when it is turned in.

The final paper in this section is a general model of an essay written in MLA format with examples of how to integrate and format quotations of prose or poetry. This model will be useful for all your Week 3 writing assignments.

In every assignment, please use MLA format (see the final model in this section, titled "MLA Format Model"). Remember to put your name, the date, the class name, and the module number and focus text title in the top left corner of each assignment you turn in. For essays or stories, also copy the assignment prompt just below this information so that you will have it handy as you are writing, and your evaluator will know exactly what question you are answering.

Note to Parents About the Model Papers

When you look at these papers, please do not panic. They are the work of some of my best students over the years, and they offer a look at what is possible, not necessarily what is routinely expected. If your student is not producing work of this caliber yet, be patient. With each completed assignment you will see growth and improvement, and that incremental growth is what you will build on. You do not have to start at the top to have good results; you just need to climb steadily!

$\backsim$

Approach Paper Format

One of my favorite tools for literary analysis is the approach paper. Although "approach paper" may seem to be an odd name for an analytical assignment, it makes sense when you realize that the exercise of writing each section of the approach paper helps to guide your thinking as you approach the essay assignment.

An approach paper consists of several sections:

I. **MLA-style heading** with your name, date, class, and name of the work you will be analyzing. (See sample for proper format.)

II. **Summary Paragraph:** A three- or four-sentence paragraph that summarizes the book or other work in as much descriptive detail as possible. Each of the sentences in your summary must begin in a different way, and sentences should be varied in length and full of interesting detail. Your writing handbook will provide specific help in sentence formatting and styling, plus guidance for correcting unclear or incomplete sentences. The summary is sometimes the most difficult section of the approach paper to write because it takes time to condense the events of the novel/play into just a few well-written sentences!

III. **Character Descriptions:** Choose and list three or four main characters in the work you are studying. In just four or five adjectives, vividly describe the character. This is a good time to use unique vocabulary words and to check the dictionary and thesaurus for ideas. Descriptive words may be used only once per approach paper, so if you use a word to describe one character, you may not use the same word to describe another character.

IV. **Discussion/Essay Questions:** Write three questions about the novel, poem, play, or essay. These questions should be thought-provoking and will almost always take more than one line to type because they ask readers to combine more than one idea. They must not be questions of fact, but of interpretation, just like the questions that are provided for your essay assignments. The act of writing this type of question helps you to think more insightfully about the characters in relationship to one another and to the setting, the author's style and intention, and the voice and reliability of the narrator. When you think seriously about these issues, you begin to approach an understanding of the text.

V. **Key Passage**: Choose the passage you feel is the most important passage in the work. This may be a brief paragraph, or it may be an entire page or more. Type it up word-for-word in the approach paper. Be sure to identify the speakers if the passage includes dialogue.

VI. **Key Passage Explanation**: In a fully developed paragraph, explain why your chosen passage is important to understanding the focus text. In your explanation make sure you integrate quotes (actual words or phrases) from the key passage to strengthen your explanation, using proper MLA format as demonstrated in your handbook or in the sample essay in this guide. Often, your chosen key passage will offer clues to the novel, poem, or play's themes. Explain any mentioned or inferred themes connected to the key passage.

Approach Paper Model

Student's Name

Date

English V: Instructor's Name

Don Quixote Approach Paper

Summary:

Don Quixote by Miguel de Cervantes is the classic tale of a Spanish madman named Don Quixote, who decides to become a knight. Along with his devoted squire Sancho Panza, Don Quixote forces himself and others into undesirable adventures throughout the Spanish nation of Castille. But Don Quixote also finds that the world does not desire a return to the old world of chivalry, for he is scorned at every turn for his desire to revive a long-lost golden age of Europe. On two different occasions, in fact, a bachelor named Sansón Carrasco (disguised as a knight-errant) tries to defeat the deluded knight in jousts, attempting to order him to return to his hometown in La Mancha. On the second attempt, Sansón defeats Don Quixote, and grants him life under the condition that he return to his home and forsake the order of knight-errantry. After Don Quixote returns home, he regains his sanity and declares, "I now abhor all profane stories of knight-errantry."

Characters

- Sancho Panza: gullible, subservient, opportunistic, acquisitive
- Don Quixote: quixotic*, idealistic, chimerical, fatuous, psychotic
- Sansón Carrasco: covetous, arrogant, avaricious, pugnacious

Discussion Questions

- The characters in *Don Quixote* make numerous references to Miguel de Cervantes himself, as though the author were a contemporary of the characters. How is the author's opinion about himself portrayed in the book? What attributes of Cervantes' own life and philosophy are expressed within the characters?

- Much of the parody in *Don Quixote* is affected by the unusual combination between knight-errantry and sixteenth-century life. How do the civilizations of Amadis of Gaul and King Arthur of England differ from Don Quixote's world?

- Cervantes makes many references to the relationship between Moors and Christians in sixteenth-century Spain. Has the relationship changed since the age when the Moors were driven out of Spain? If so, how?

Key Passage, from Chapter XV of Book II, p. 627

In his first joust with Sansón Carrasco, Don Quixote emerges victorious from battle and elated with joy over his triumph. Afterward, the following passage ensues:

> Carrasco undertook the task [to defeat Don Quixote in a joust], and Tomé Cecial, Sancho's comrade and neighbor, a merry, scatterbrained fellow, offered his services as squire. Sansón armed himself as has been described and Tomé Cecial, to avoid being recognized by his comrade when they met, fitted on over his natural nose the false one already mentioned. And so they followed the same road as Don Quixote and very nearly reached him in time to be present at the adventure of the cart of Death, and at last they met in the wood, where everything that the extraordinary fancies of Don Quixote, who took it into his head that the bachelor was not the bachelor, Master Bachelor licentiate, because he did not find nests where he expected to find birds. Tomé Cecial, seeing how badly their plans had turned out and what a wretched end their expedition had come to, said to the bachelor: "For sure, Master Sansón Carrasco, we've met with our deserts. It is easy to plan and start an enterprise, but most times it

is hard to get out of it safe and sound. Don Quixote is mad, and we are sane, but he comes off safe and in high spirits, while you, master, are left drubbed and downcast. Tell us, now, who is the greater madman, he who is so because he cannot help it, or he who is so of his own free will?"

Key Passage Explanation:

This passage offers a panoramic view of the whole paradox of Don Quixote. Don Quixote is mad, but the sane madness of his opponents is even worse, for in their depravity they are mad of their "own free will." We see in this passage that everyone is a sort of villain in this book. Don Quixote meets with his own hardships, but as Tomé Cecial points out, "We've met with our own deserts [deserved punishments]." Cervantes does not advocate the false chivalry promulgated in the books of knight-errantry, but neither does he support its alternative. By ridiculing both extremes, Cervantes tacitly expresses his desire for a balance.

⌒

Historical Approach Paper Format

Event or Era

Place

Time

Event Summary

Write an interesting one-paragraph summary of the period or event.

Key Players

Choose 3–4 key people involved in the event, and list 4–5 vividly descriptive words for each person. Words may not be used to describe more than one character.

Discussion Questions

Think carefully about the event, and write three analytical discussion questions.

Turning Point

Choose an event that seems to mark a significant turning point or climax in the period or event, and write a one-paragraph description.

Why do you believe this was a significant turning point? What happened afterward? Write a fully developed paragraph explaining your choice. Support your argument with quotes from the text or other sources, if appropriate.

⤙

Historical Approach Paper Model

Student's Name

Date

English I: Instructor's Name

Event: Russian Revolution

Place: Russia

Time: 1917

Event/Era Summary

The Russian Revolution was not a single event in which Tsar Nicholas II was defeated and removed from power, but a broad expression of two events, the February Revolution and the October Revolution. Leading up to the February Revolution, Russia experienced turmoil and political conflict over issues such as the country's economic condition and its prevailing failure in World War I. Conditions in Russia continued to worsen until a festival in one of Russia's prominent cities turned into a large protest, inducing Nicholas II to order a military intervention which proved futile, as much of his military was no longer loyal. This event caused Nicholas II to resign the position of tsar to his brother, Michael Alexandrovich, who was not willing to serve without election. Without anyone to fill the position, Russia had no other choice than to set up a temporary government, eventually headed by Alexander Kerensky. Another important character, Vladimir Lenin, plays a significant role in the October Revolution as a member of the communist revolution with a plan to overthrow the current government. Lenin's plan worked to perfection as military guards laid down their arms immediately without resistance. Alexander Kerensky soon fled the palace and the new government, led by Lenin, took effect.

Key Players

- Tsar Nicholas II: obstinate, neglectful, destructive, intelligent
- Vladimir Lenin: persuasive, radical, visionary, rebellious
- Alexander Kerensky: popular, successful, convincing, renowned

Discussion Questions

I. Though it may have been due to his lack of political education, Nicholas II made many mistakes as a leader. What measures could he have taken in an attempt to avoid the widespread upheaval that occurred?

II. Why was Vladimir Lenin so successful in spreading the principles of Marxism? Did the people find hope in his ideas when it seemed as if there was no hope?

III. How did conditions change in Russia after the Revolution of 1917? In what ways did relations with other countries change?

Turning Point

Forced by the growing pressure to turn the economic momentum around and by overall unpopularity, Tsar Nicholas II stepped out of office. He gave his leadership role to his younger brother; however, he would not accept it without the vote of the people. Out of necessity the Russian Provisional Government was assembled in Petrograd to form some type of leadership.

Turing Point Explanation

The time of the resignation of Tsar Nicholas II is the first radical change of the Russian Revolution, but it also marks the end of tsarist rule in Russia. This created a need for a political change to sustain the government, leading into the Russian Provisional Government. Although this occurred during the February Revolution, these events allowed the happenings of the October Revolution to take place, thus completing the entire Revolution of 1917. This time period is a turning point because it started the transformation and provided an outlet for the following events to occur. Without these events it would have been extremely difficult for Lenin and his followers to procure leadership.

Author Profile Format

For each focus work it is important to complete an Author Profile. If you cannot find the recommended biography in your local library, feel free to substitute any short biography that you find. I suggest using biographies found in the middle-grade or young adult sections of the library, as they usually provide an adequate introduction to the author's life without dwelling unnecessarily on the less savory bits.

Name (including pseudonyms if any)

  Birth Date   **Place**

  Death Date   **Place**

Best-Known Works

  Include three or more of the author's best or best-known works.

Brief Biography

- How does this author use his or her personal experiences in his or her work?
- What current events or public figures affected the author's life and writing?
- How do the places in the author's life show up in his or her writing?

Author Profile Model

Name: Washington Irving (pseudonyms include Dietrich Knickerbocker, Jonathan Oldstyle, and Geoffrey Crayon)

  Birth Date: April 3, 1783 **Place:** Manhattan, NYC, NY

  Death Date: November 28, 1859 **Place:** Sunnyside, Irvington, NY

Best-Known Works

- *The Legend of Sleepy Hollow, Rip Van Winkle, The Sketchbook of Geoffrey Crayon, The Life of George Washington, Knickerbocker's History of New York*

Brief Biography

Washington Irving used his experiences living in both Europe and America to write humorous and meditative stories popular in both the new and old worlds. Irving's life and work were influenced by the events of the Revolutionary War and the War of 1812, and he was also profoundly influenced by other writers (both European and American) of his time. His favorite childhood stories involved voyages to far-off lands. The places of Irving's life show up extensively in his writing. He wrote of England, America, and even lived in Tarrytown, New York, where he set *The Legend of Sleepy Hollow*.

⌐

Literature Summary Format

Novel or Story Title: Write the story's full title and subtitle, if any, here.

Author: Write the author's full name and pseudonym, if any.

Theme: What is the main idea that the author wants to convey? The theme is the big idea illustrated by the story's plot and characters. This can often be expressed in a proverb or phrase such as "honesty is the best policy" or "love never fails."

Characterization: WHO is the story about, and what are they like? How does the author show you this?

Plot: WHAT happens in the story?

Setting: WHEN and WHERE does the story take place?

Style: HOW does the author create a mood and tell the story?

⌐

Literature Summary Model

Novel or Story Title: "The Secret Life of Walter Mitty"

Author: James Thurber

Theme

"The Secret Life of Walter Mitty" explores the desire of every human being to be smarter, braver, and more important, and what happens when this fantasy world becomes an addiction more real than reality itself.

Characterization

Walter Mitty is humanity taken to an extreme. He is a daydreamer, imagining he is a Navy pilot flying through the most devastating hurricane in history when he is just driving his wife to her hair appointment, or envisioning himself as a world-renowned surgeon when he drives past a hospital. You also get the feeling that Walter may be aging and not "all there."

Plot

"The Secret Life of Walter Mitty" chronicles a day in Mitty's life and his struggles to complete his daily routine instead of slipping into his fantasy world.

Setting

The setting of 1940s England has very little effect on the story, except that certain buildings Mitty passes do occasionally prompt certain daydreams.

Style

The story is handled with a rather straightforward, simple style that changes for each daydream. For example, when he imagines himself as a combat pilot, the characters speak with an efficient, clipped style, using only as many words as are necessary.

Literary Analysis Model

This model corresponds with the instructions found in the chapters on "How to Read a Book" and "How to Write an Essay." You will find this model helpful for most of the essays assigned throughout the curriculum. Additional models can be found in the Excellence in Literature *Handbook for Writers*.

Student Name

Date

Class Name

Module # and Focus Text Title

Prompt

Pride and Prejudice was originally titled *First Impressions*. Consider both titles in relation to the characters of Elizabeth, Darcy, and Mr. Wickham, as well as to Austen's depiction of social class. What are the roles of pride, prejudice, and first impressions in the development of relationships among these characters and their social circles? What does Austen seem to suggest about pride, prejudice, and first impressions? Be sure to note Austen's use of irony, and provide specific textual support for your thesis.

The Defects of Human Nature

Life in the early 1800s revolved primarily around the social aspects of life. Social conventions ruled the actions of young ladies and their mothers, guided their brothers in selecting a spouse, and even dictated with whom their families were permitted to associate. Jane Austen gently ridicules the rigid structure of her society's rules and regimens in her novel *Pride and Prejudice*. Through her ironic situations and comical views of life, she attempts to reveal some of society's faults and offer alternatives for the faulty tendencies of human nature.

Pride was an integral part of the nineteenth-century culture. At the very foundation of the separations between social classes, pride enabled entire families to choose not to associate with each other so as not to damage their own social reputations. Mr. Darcy, "a fine figure of a man" with "ten thousand [pounds] a year" (16), embodied this pride admirably. During the first ball he attended in Hertfordshire, his air of superiority proved that he was assuredly aware that his fortune was much larger than anyone's in the room and that his social status was accordingly higher. His reclusive nature and manners also added to the aura of pride which enveloped him.

Although his neighbors were gentlemen and gentlemen's daughters, Mr. Darcy believed that his income and social standing in London set him above the residents of Hertfordshire. Indeed, later he acknowledged that his parents "almost taught [him] to be selfish and overbearing—to care for none beyond [his] own family circle, to think meanly of all the rest of the world, to wish at least to think meanly of their sense and worth compared with [his] own" (274).

Mr. Darcy further displayed the pride which was so deeply ingrained in him when he bungled his first proposal to Elizabeth Bennet. Although he began acceptably with expressions of his love, "he was not more eloquent on the subject of tenderness than of pride" (149). The descriptions of his admiration soon turned to illustrations of the obstacles he overcame to stand before her and propose. Despite his intended purpose to depict the depth of his emotion, his expressions of "his sense of her inferiority ... of the family obstacles which judgment had always opposed to inclination" (149) only served to anger and insult Elizabeth. Mr. Darcy's pride prevented him from understanding that the differences in social standing were evident to Elizabeth and that she would not be flattered by his explanations.

Although Elizabeth was not proud in the same manner as Mr. Darcy, she was not immune to human faults. Elizabeth's flaw was expressed in the more socially acceptable form of prejudice. Elizabeth discovered the danger of relying on first impressions as her relationships with Mr. Darcy developed. Mr. Darcy's actions at their first meeting prompted her to accept her community's harsh opinion of him as her own. Without making the effort to get to know Mr. Darcy, Elizabeth fixed her own views about his character and held "no very cordial feelings towards him" (17).

Elizabeth then repeated her mistake of allowing her impressions to turn into prejudice when she met Mr. Wickham. "… Struck with [Mr. Wickham's] air" (63) she formed her acquaintance with an inclination to approve of his actions. This inclination caused her to believe Mr. Wickham explicitly when he fabricated tales about Mr. Darcy. It reached to the extent that her friend felt the need to advise her not to "allow her fancy for Wickham to make her appear unpleasant in the eyes of a man of ten times his consequence" (77).

Ironically, Elizabeth did not begin to alter her prejudices until she accused Mr. Darcy of causing Mr. Wickham's "misfortune" (150). Mr. Darcy's account of the matters forced her to reverse her opinions about him and Mr. Wickham. "Every lingering struggle in [Mr. Wickham's] favor grew fainter and fainter" (161) as she recognized his indecent behavior and consequently scolded herself for not identifying them sooner. This discovery of the true character of these gentlemen was humiliating to Elizabeth as she had "prided [herself] on [her] discernment" (162). However painful this lesson may have been, Elizabeth benefited from it by gaining insight into the hazards of prejudice.

Although Jane Austen first titled her novel *First Impressions*, her final choice of *Pride and Prejudice* seems to fit her analysis of human behavior more suitably. Her humorous novel prodded her contemporaries to formulate their own opinions and not to rely on society's poor abilities or their own preconceived notions about themselves. It forced their descendants to confront their own human nature and face their personal defects.

⤳

Sample Poetry Analysis Model

Student Name

Date

Class Name

Module # and Focus Text Title

Prompt: Make a close reading of "God's Grandeur" or "The Windhover" by Gerard Manley Hopkins. Make sure you show how the images and figurative language in the poem complement one another. Show also how he uses sound, including consonance, assonance, and rhyme in constructing his poetic argument. Consider also how he develops his poetic argument from the beginning to the end of his poem.

Inspired by a Falcon

In "The Windhover," Gerard Manley Hopkins talks about watching a kestrel, a small falcon which hovers in the air. Dedicated to Christ, this poem celebrates the majesty, beauty, and power of one of God's creations. Hopkins describes the kestrel's flight, hovering, and dive, as well as his reaction to this display of strength. He is clearly awed, for "[his] heart …Stirred for a bird" (7–8).

Hopkins uses figurative language and imagery throughout "The Windhover." The title itself conveys the image of the kestrel hovering in the wind. In addition, the sounds of the poem correspond with its action.

In the first stanza Hopkins describes the kestrel's steady flying and gliding, as well as the poet's own admiration. The poem begins with "I caught this morning morning's minion, king- / dom of daylight's dauphin, dapple-dawn-drawn Falcon," (1–2).

The word "caught" is used figuratively, as in seen. The word "minion" means darling, and "Dauphin" is the title for the prince who is the heir to the French throne; Hopkins is acknowledging that the kestrel is the darling and ruler of the daylight. He admires "the achieve of, the mastery of the thing!" (7–8), as the kestrel flies uninhibited, master of flying and the air. Hopkins's use of the words "riding" (2) and "striding" (3) help us to see the image of the kestrel flying through the air. In addition, these words give us a sense of the kestrel moving smoothly with a sense of rhythm, which meshes well with his later image of skating. The kestrel glides or hovers through the air, just "As a skate's heel sweeps smooth on a bow-bend" (6).

This stanza has a rhythm that swings along, heightened by alliteration, assonance, and consonance, as in "dapple-dawn-drawn[.]" Later in the stanza Hopkins uses alliteration again to produce a smooth sound that imitates gliding. In addition, the way every line rhymes (they all end with "-ing") also emphasizes rhythm.

In the next stanza Hopkins is talking about the kestrel flying up and then diving down. He uses figurative language to convey the action. "Brute beauty and valour and act, oh, air, pride, plume, here / Buckle! AND the fire that breaks from thee" (9–10). Hopkins describes the kestrel by its attributes, and the combined effect is an impression of soaring and climbing. The bird is not "valour and act … air, pride, plume," but it and its flight embody those ideas. "Buckle!" and its possible meanings are a one-word summary of what is happening: to get ready, to make fast, to fall through. The poem builds up speed and dives with the windhover. Hopkins uses lots of different consonants and vowels to create a jumbled sound of words climbing upon one another, building up to "Buckle!" just as the kestrel climbs up and then dives. The "fire that breaks from [the kestrel]" refers to the way the kestrel's wings flash open, revealing a reddish-brown color, as the bird nears the ground. Later in the stanza Hopkins refers to the windhover as a "chevalier" (11), which conveys the idea of nobility and strength and "valour" (9). A knight gallops across the countryside; the kestrel hovers and dives in the sky.

In the last stanza the poem flies swiftly and easily to the ground with the bird. This stanza is more quiet; Hopkins uses soft-sounding vowels and consonants. "Sheer plod make plough down sillion / Shine" (12–13) has smooth consonants that move steadily forward just like a plow. Hopkins compares this to the way the kestrel plows through the air. Matching with the earlier figurative language of fire, Hopkins presents an image of "blue-bleak embers, ah my dear, [that] / Fall, gall themselves, and gash gold-vermilion." The embers are falling, opening, and glowing. This helps us to see the image of the kestrel diving through the sky and flashing open his reddish-brown wings when he nears the ground, just as the embers "gash gold-vermilion." In the last line, "Fall, gall themselves, and gash gold-vermilion" (14), even though the g's are hard, the vowel sounds; particularly the use of ah (definitely an example of assonance), soften the line.

Throughout "The Windhover," Hopkins's awe is evident in his enthusiastic description. He conveys his message with words and sounds that echo and emphasize his story, making it a poem of both visual images and oral expression. He uses this method to involve and engage the reader in his experience. Hopkins's soaring poetry shares his awe of the kestrel and its Creator with the reader.

～

MLA Format Model

Use these format guidelines for all assignments.

Your Name

Date

Class Name

Module # and Focus Text Title

For an EIL essay, please add the writing prompt at this point.

Making Your Essay Look Good:

The Basics of MLA Format

In the upper right-hand corner of each page, beginning with page two if you prefer, one-half inch from the top (the text of your essay should begin one inch from the top), place a header with your last name, a space, and the page number. In most word-processing programs, you can do this from the "View" menu by selecting "Header and Footer." [NOTE: This is not shown in these models, but should be done in your own essays.] You should have one-inch margins on the right, the left, and the bottom of your page, and your essay should be double-spaced (set line spacing in your word processing program—do *not* place a hard return at the end of each line). Use one space at the end of terminal punctuation.

When you quote poetry, if the quotation is three or fewer lines, fit it right into your text. For instance, if I want to let you know that Blake begins "The Ecchoing Green" by juxtaposing "merry bells [that] ring / To welcome the spring" and "The sky-lark and thrush, / The birds of the bush," I would do it like I just did it. I might also note that Blake emphasizes this juxtaposition by the rhyme of "ring" and "sing," a rhyme that helps connect the natural and the human worlds because the sound describing the voices of the birds in the green echoes the sound describing the voice of human-made bells.

Notice that I keep the punctuation and the upper-case letters as they are in the poem. If I want to add something to make the quotation fit the grammar of my sentence, I do so by indicating the addition with brackets. If I wanted to leave something out of the poem and pick up the quotation a few words later, I would use ellipses, which are three dots with spaces between them (. . .).

I might then want to point out that, while "Old John" chimes in to the "merry" sounds as he "laugh[s] away care," the second stanza of the poem suggests his aging, and thus his experience of life, which might subtly trouble the innocence of the green. To show my point, I might quote the first five lines of the second stanza, though I might then find myself drifting from the close attention required in a solid analysis. If I take that chance of inattention, I would indent each line ten spaces and reproduce the lines of the poem just as they appear in the text. I would do this because I am quoting four or more lines of poetry. So the quotation would look like this:

> Old John with white hair
>
> Does laugh away care,
>
> Sitting under the oak,
>
> Among the old folk.
>
> They laugh at our play, . . .

After this, I had better make some particular observations about the language of the excerpt that I just quoted.

Remember, your essay's title is not the same as the title of the work you discuss in the essay. Your title has no quotation marks unless you have a quotation in it; neither is it underlined. Use quotation marks for the title of a short poem, essay, or short story. Italicize (or underline) the title of a book, a play, or a long poem—Wordsworth's *Prelude*, for instance.

In quoting prose, if the quotation takes up more than three lines of your text, you should indent the entire block ten spaces. Do not use ellipses (three periods separated by spaces) at the beginning or the end of the quotation; use them in the middle of the quotation to indicate you have removed words that are not essential to your point. Be sure to introduce all quotations with appropriate tags, blending quotations into your own sentence structure, grammar, and syntax. Punctuate quotations and cite page numbers as I do in the following sentence: DuBois begins his essay by depicting and defining the internalized "contempt and pity" of African-American "double-consciousness" (38); he ends the essay by turning that contempt and pity back upon the white America, a "dusty desert of dollars and smartness" (43). Notice that the end punctuation follows the page citation and is not within the quotation itself. Notice also that only the page number is within the parentheses. I would include an author's name only if the particular author was not clear from context.

If you have further questions about MLA style, look in the library for a copy of the *MLA Handbook for Writers of Research Papers,* use a writing handbook such as the Excellence in Literature *Handbook for Writers*, or visit the website below.

https://owl.english.purdue.edu/owl/resource/747/01/

Note: *This sample essay was provided courtesy of Dr. Robert Grotjohn, Professor Emeritus of English, Mary Baldwin College. It was one of the most helpful documents I received while in college, and I used it as a model for nearly every essay I wrote. I hope you find it equally helpful.*

How to Evaluate Writing

Let your speech be always with grace . . .

—Colossians 4:6

A constructive evaluation measures the student's work against an objective standard and assesses where and how the work meets or exceeds the standard, and what needs improvement. Always remember to evaluate skills from high to low, evaluating Content standards (Ideas/Concepts and Organization) first, then Style standards (Voice, Sentence Fluency, and Word Choice), and finally, Mechanics (Conventions and Presentation).

If a student has many significant areas of difficulty, evaluate only the skills that have been specifically taught. Be sure the student knows how to consult a writer's handbook and the formats and models in this guide for questions of structure, style, or usage. Use the numbered sections in the handbook, along with the rubric, to provide constructive, instructional feedback. Even students who begin the year with difficulty tend to catch up as they progress through the course and learn by repeatedly going through the read/think/write/evaluate/revise/evaluate cycle throughout the year.

How to Use a Writer's Handbook for Instructive Evaluation

A good writer's handbook makes it easy to offer specific, constructive feedback. If you have used a handbook such as *Writers INC* or the Excellence in Literature

Handbook for Writers, you know that information is categorized into numbered paragraphs. These numbers allow you to direct the student to exactly the instruction he or she needs to fix an error or improve a skill.

For example, if your student is having difficulty with subject/verb agreement, you would look in the table of contents of the *Handbook for Writers* and find that subject/verb agreement appears in section 1.8 on page 242. On the student's paper, note the section number so that the student can visit the handbook, read the paragraph, look at the examples, and see how to correct the error. It is quick and efficient, and best of all, much more helpful than just telling the student to be sure that the subject and verb agree.

How to Evaluate the First Draft

After you do an initial read-through of the student's rough draft, get your writer's handbook and a copy of the rubric and evaluate the two Content skills, Ideas and Concepts and Organization.

I realize it is counter-intuitive for many parents to evaluate only the Content standards, because you will see mechanical errors or style problems in the rough draft. However, until the content and organization of the piece are finalized, there is little point in tweaking word choice or sentence fluency. Working only with content helps keep attention on the first draft priorities of ideas and organization, and avoids the distraction of too much red ink.

How to Evaluate a Final Draft

When you receive a revised draft, read through it quickly to gain an overall impression. Have the changes you discussed in the previous draft been satisfactorily made? Use a fresh copy of the rubric to assess each of the seven skill areas and provide a feedback number or symbol for each characteristic listed.

For each draft, return the student's paper with a filled-out rubric, a brief note highlighting the positive and negative things you noticed about the paper, and handbook section numbers so the student can look up challenging items.

Should You Require More than Two Drafts?

Two drafts—a first and a final—are all I recommend. Writing skills improve with each new assignment, and moving through the assignments in a timely manner ensures that students will not get bogged down and end up disliking one of the classics.

This section adapted from *Evaluate Writing the Easy Way* by Janice Campbell.

Excellence in Literature Evaluation Rubric

Name: Assignment:	Date: Evaluator:

Content: Ideas and Concepts

_ The essay contains a strong, easily identified thesis.
_ Interesting ideas and a compelling perspective hold the reader's attention.
_ Relevant anecdotes, appropriate quotes, and specific details support the writer's position and demonstrate understanding of the prompt.

Content: Organization

_ The structure of the paper enhances the presentation of the thesis and supporting ideas.
_ Clear transitions move the reader easily from idea to idea.
_ Quotes and textual support are blended smoothly, with correct tenses and formatting.

Style: Voice

_ The writer speaks directly to the reader, using an appropriate tone and level of formality.
_ The writer's voice is individual and engaging, providing a sense of the writer's personality.
_ The writer demonstrates awareness of and respect for the audience and purpose of the writing.

Mechanics: Conventions

_ Standard writing conventions (spelling, punctuation, capitalization, grammar, usage, paragraphing) are observed.
_ Citations are correctly formatted using the MLA standard.
_ Mechanical or typographical errors are few; only minor touch-ups needed.

Style: Sentence Fluency

_ Sentences flow easily with graceful transitions.
_ Sentences have a pleasant, appropriate rhythm and cadence when read aloud.
_ Sentence structure is varied, with appropriate use of simple, complex, and compound sentences.

Mechanics: Presentation

_ Essay is in MLA format: Times-New Roman font, 12 pt., 1" margins.
_ Paper header with student, class, instructor, and date included.
_ Essay prompt included after header and before title.
_ Single space following all terminal punctuation.

Style: Word Choice

_ Chosen words clearly convey the intended message.
_ The words used are precise, interesting, powerful, engaging, and natural.
_ The vocabulary is vivid and varied, though not necessarily exotic.

Comments and Handbook Lookups

Rating Scale

5 or + indicates that your essay demonstrated outstanding mastery in this area.
4 indicates that the essay is above average.
3 or = indicates that your essay was average and met assignment expectations in this area.
2 indicates that your essay was below average in this area.
1 or - indicates that you should write down this skill as a goal area for improvement.

Glossary

Allegory: A story in which ideas are represented or personified as actions, people, or things. Example: *Pilgrim's Progress* by John Bunyan.

Alliteration: The repetition of beginning consonant sounds through a sequence of words. Gerard Manley Hopkins is noted for using alliteration in lines such as "Fresh-firecoal chestnut-falls; finches' wings;" from "Pied Beauty."

Allude/Allusion: To make a reference, either implied or stated, to the Bible, mythology, literature, art, music, or history that relies on the reader's familiarity with the alluded-to work to make or reinforce a point in the current work.

Analogy: A comparison based upon similarities and relationships of things that are somewhat alike but mostly different. An analogy often makes a point-by-point comparison from a familiar object to an unfamiliar.

Antagonist: The character who opposes the main character (the protagonist).

Antithesis: A counter-proposition that denotes a direct contrast to the original proposition, balancing an argument for parallel structure.

Archetype: A plot pattern, such as the quest or the redeemer/scapegoat, or character element, such as the cruel stepmother, that recurs across cultures.

Assonance: The repetition of vowel sounds in a series of words. Example: "The rain in Spain falls mainly on the plain" from *Pygmalion* by George Bernard Shaw.

Ballad: A narrative poem or song with a repeating refrain. A ballad often tells the story of a historical event or retells a folk legend. Example: "The Raven" by Edgar Allen Poe.

Beast Fable: Also known as a "beast epic," this is an often satirical, allegorical style in which the main characters are animals. It is often written as a mock epic. Example: *Animal Farm* by George Orwell.

Blank Verse: Unrhymed poetry, usually iambic pentameter.

Burlesque: Refers to ridiculous exaggeration in language, usually one that makes the discrepancy between the words and the situation or the character silly. For example, to have a king speak like an idiot or a workman speak like a king (especially, say, in blank verse) is burlesque. Similarly, a very serious situation can be burlesqued by having the characters in it speak or behave in ridiculously inappropriate ways. In other words, burlesque creates a large gap between the situation or the characters and the style with which they speak or act out the event.

Caricature: The technique of exaggerating for comic and satiric effect one particular feature of a subject, in order to achieve a grotesque or ridiculous effect. Caricatures can be created either through words or pictures.

Characterization: The artistic presentation of a fictional character.

Citation: A standardized reference to a source of information in a written work. The citation usually includes author, title, publisher, and so forth, in a specific format. In the MLA style of citation that we use with this curriculum, the citations appear as signal phrases in the body of the text, and a "works cited" list follows the text.

Climax: The turning point in fiction; the transition from rising to falling action.

Comedy: In literary terms a comedy is a story, often centered on love, that has a positive ending. It may or may not be humorous.

Conflict: A struggle between two opposing forces. The conflict usually forms the central drama in a fictional narrative, and can be man vs. man, man vs. God, man vs. nature, man vs. society, or even man vs. himself.

Consonance: An "almost rhyme" in which consonants agree, but the vowels that precede them differ. Example: word/lord, slip/slop.

Couplet: In poetry, a pair of rhyming lines often appearing at the end of a sonnet.

Denouement: Resolution or conclusion.

Diction: An author's word choices.

Didactic: Literature with a moralistic or instructive purpose.

Elegy: A poem, usually written as a formal lament on the death of a person. In classical time an elegy was any poem written in elegiac meter. Example: "In Memory of W. B. Yeats" by W. H. Auden.

End Rhyme: The repetition of identical or similar sounds in two or more different words found at the end of poetic lines.

Epic: A long narrative poem that tells a story, usually about the deeds of a hero. Example: Beowulf.

Epigram: A brief saying or poem, often ironic or satirical.

Epigraph: A phrase, quotation, or poem that suggests something about the theme and is set at the beginning of a chapter or book.

Epistolary Style: A novel composed of a series of letters.

Essay: A paper that takes a position on a topic.

Euphemism: The substitution of a socially acceptable word or expression in place of harsh or unacceptable language. Example: "Passed away" for "died."

Exposition: The part of the narrative structure in which the scene is set, characters introduced, and the situation established. It usually falls at the beginning of the book, but additional exposition is often scattered throughout the work.

Fable: A short story, usually featuring animals or other non-human characters, that illustrates a moral lesson. Example: Aesop's "The Crow and the Pitcher."

Falling Action: The portion of plot structure, usually following the climax, in which the problems encountered during the rising action are solved.

Figure of Speech: A comparison in which something is pictured or figured in other more familiar terms. See simile and metaphor.

Flashback: A plot device in which a scene from the fictional past is brought into the fictional present, often to explain or illustrate a character's next action.

Foot: A group of syllables that form a basic unit of poetic rhythm.

Foreshadow: Hints or clues about future events in a narrative.

Framed Narrative: A story or stories told within a narrative frame. Example: *The Canterbury Tales* by Geoffrey Chaucer. Chaucer has framed a vivid grouping of stories within the frame of a narrative about a group of pilgrims who are traveling to Canterbury.

Free Verse: Poetry that does not rhyme, has no set line length, and is not set to traditional meter.

Full Stop: A period or other punctuation mark that indicates the end of a sentence.

Genre: A category of classification for literature such as fiction, non-fiction, and so forth. Pronounced zhahn-ruh.

Gothic Novel: A genre that evokes an aura of mystery and may include ghosts, dark and stormy nights, isolated castles, and supernatural happenings. Example: *Wuthering Heights* by Emily Brontë or *Frankenstein* by Mary Shelley.

Handbook: A writer's handbook such as the *Handbook for Writers* from Excellence in Literature, *Write for College, Writer's Inc.* from Write Source, or *Writer's Reference* by Diana Hacker.

Heroic Couplet: Two rhymed lines in iambic pentameter, forming a complete thought. This form was often used by Alexander Pope.

Homonym/Homophone: Words that sound much the same but have different meanings, origins, or spelling.

Hubris: A term derived from the Greek language that means excessive pride. In Greek tragedy and mythology, hubris often leads to the hero's downfall.

Hyperbole: Overstatement through exaggerated language.

Imagery: Words, phrases, and sensory details used to create a mood or mental picture in a reader's mind. Example: From "Mariana" by Alfred, Lord Tennyson:
"With blackest moss the flower-plots
Were thickly crusted, one and all;
The rusted nails fell from the knots
That held the pear to the gable wall.
The broken sheds looked sad and strange:
Unlifted was the clinking latch;
Weeded and worth the ancient thatch

Upon the lonely moated grange . . . "

Iambic Pentameter: In poetry, a metrical pattern in a ten-syllable line of verse in which five unaccented syllables alternate with five accented syllables, with the accent usually falling on the second of each pair of syllables.

Irony: A stylistic device or figure of speech in which the real meaning of the words is different from (and opposite to) the literal meaning. Irony, unlike sarcasm, tends to be ambiguous, bringing two contrasting meanings into play.

Manners: A novel of manners focuses on and describes in detail the social customs and habits of a particular social group. Examples include *Pride and Prejudice* by Jane Austen and *Age of Innocence* by Edith Wharton.

Metaphor: A comparison between two objects, not using the terms "like" or "as."

Meter: The pattern of stressed and unstressed syllables in a line of poetry.

Mock Heroic: A satiric style which sets up a deliberately disproportionate and witty distance between the elevated language used to describe an action or event and the triviality or foolishness of the action (using, for example, the language of epics to describe a tea party). The mock heroic style tends to be an inside joke, in that it appeals to the sophistication of a reader familiar with the epic original but is not understood by readers who are not familiar with the traditional epic form. It encourages the reader to see the ridiculousness of the heroic pretensions of trivial people and is thus an excellent vehicle for skewering the sin of pride. Example: "Mac Flecknoe" by John Dryden or Pope's "Rape of the Lock."

Motif: A recurrent device, formula, or situation, often connecting a fresh idea with common patterns of existing thought.

Myth: A type of story that is usually symbolic and extensive, including stories shared across a culture to explain its history and traditions. Example: "Romulus and Remus."

Narrator: The character who tells the story. This may or may not be the hero, and the narrator may be reliable or unreliable. Example: Ishmael in *Moby Dick*.

Nature: As it refers to a person, this is used to identify something inborn or inherent, such as the "old nature" of Scripture, that often leads to predictable actions.

Octave: In poetry, the first eight lines of the Italian, or Petrarchan, sonnet.

Ode: A lyric poem with a serious topic and formal tone but without formal pattern. This form was especially popular among the Romantic poets. Example: "Ode to the West Wind" by Percy Bysshe Shelley.

Omniscient Point of View: In literature, a narrative perspective from multiple points of view that gives the reader access to the thoughts of all the characters.

Onomatopoeia: The formation or use of a word that sounds like what it means. Example: hiss; sizzle; pop.

Oxymoron: A figure of speech that combines two seemingly contradictory elements. Example: living death; sweet sorrow.

Parable: A short story with an explicit moral lesson. Example: The parable of the sower (Matthew 13:18–30).

Paradox: A statement that may appear contradictory but is actually true. Example: "Less is more."

Parody: A style of writing that deliberately seeks to ridicule another style, primarily through exaggeration.

Pastoral: Poem or play that describes an idealized, simple life that country folk, usually shepherds, are imagined to live in a world full of beauty, music, and love.

Personification: To endow a non-human object with human qualities. Example: Death in "Death Be Not Proud" by John Donne.

Picaresque: A style of novel that features a loosely connected series of events, rather than a tightly constructed plot, often with a non-traditional hero. Example: *Moll Flanders* by Daniel Defoe.

Plagiarism: To plagiarize is to copy or borrow the work or ideas of another author without acknowledgment. It is both unethical and illegal. When you are writing anything, such as essays, reports, dissertations, or creative works, you must cite your sources of information, including books, periodicals, or online resources, within your text as well as in a list of references appended to the work.

Plot: The sequence of narrated events that form a story.

Poetic Justice: A literary device in which virtue is ultimately rewarded or vice punished.

Point of View: The perspective from which people, events, and other details in a story are viewed.

Protagonist: The main character in a work, either male or female.

Pseudonym: A false name used to disguise a writer's identity. Example: Mary Anne Evans used the pseudonym George Eliot.

Pun: A wordplay that exploits the double meaning or ambiguity in a word to create an amusing effect. Example: The title of *The Importance of Being Earnest* by Oscar Wilde.

Quest: A type of literary plot that focuses on a protagonist's journey toward a difficult goal. There may or may not be a physical journey involved. Example: Homer's *Odyssey*; J. R. R. Tolkien's *The Lord of the Rings*.

Realism: A type of literature that tries to present life as it really is.

Reductio ad absurdum: A popular satiric technique in which the author agrees enthusiastically with the basic attitudes or assumptions he wishes to satirize and, by pushing them to a logically ridiculous extreme, exposes the foolishness of the original attitudes and assumptions. Example: "A Modest Proposal" by Jonathan Swift.

Refrain: A phrase, line, or group of lines that is repeated throughout a poem, usually after every stanza.

Resolution: The point of closure to the conflict in the plot.

Rhetoric: The art of using language to persuade or influence others. Sometimes includes the idea of eloquence (an older meaning) or of insincerity or artificiality in language (more modern interpretation). Examples: Mark Antony's speech in *Julius Caesar* by William Shakespeare or the character of Squealer in *Animal Farm* by George Orwell.

Rhyme Scheme: The pattern of end rhymes in a poem, noted by small letters, e.g., abab or abcba, etc.

Rising Action: The part of the plot structure in which events complicate or intensify the conflict, or introduce additional conflict.

Romance: A type of novel that presents an idealized picture of life. A novel of romance can be considered almost the opposite of a novel of realism. If you were expecting that the definition of "romance" would have something to do with love, you may want to look at the definition of "comedy" instead.

Rubric: A checklist for scoring that includes guidelines for expectations.

Sarcasm: A form of verbal irony in which apparent praise is actually criticism. Example: "A modest little person, with much to be modest about." Winston Churchill

Satire: A composition in verse or prose that uses humor, irony, sarcasm, or ridicule to point out vice or folly in order to expose, discourage, and change morally offensive attitudes or behaviors. It has been aptly described as an attack with a smile. Example: "A Modest Proposal" by Jonathan Swift.

Scansion: The process of analytically scanning a poem line by line to determine its meter.

Setting: The time and place in which the action of a story, poem, or play takes place.

Simile: A comparison of two things, using the words "like" or "as." Example: "My love is like a red, red rose . . . " by Robert Burns.

Soliloquy: A monologue in which a character talks to himself. Example: Hamlet's "To be or not to be . . . " soliloquy.

Sonnet: A fixed verse form consisting of fourteen lines, usually in iambic pentameter. Variations include Italian (Petrarchan), Shakespearean, and Spenserian.

Stanza: A section of a poem, preceded and followed by an extra line space.

Stereotype: A characterization based on the assumption that a personal trait such as gender, age, ethnic or national identity, religion, occupation, or marital status is predictably accompanied by certain characteristics, actions, even values.

Stock Character: A flat character sketch that fills a classic, easily understood role without much detail. Example: The wicked stepmother in *Cinderella*.

Stream of Consciousness: A modern writing style that replicates and records the random flow of thoughts, emotions, memories, and associations as they rush through a character's mind. Example: *To the Lighthouse* by Virginia Woolf.

Structure: The arrangement of the various elements in a work.

Style: A distinctive manner of expression distinguished by the writer's diction, rhythm, imagery, and so on.

Syllabus: An outline of course requirements. In *Excellence in Literature*, the syllabus is this book in its entirety.

Symbol: A person, place, thing, event, or pattern in a literary work that is not only itself but also stands for something else, often something more abstract. Common symbolism includes darkness as a representation of confusion or evil; a storm as foreboding or a threat; or beauty as a symbol of virtue. This PDF may help you understand symbols: http://goo.gl/gGLU4O

Textual Support: Brief quotes from a text that is being analyzed. These quotes should usually be smoothly integrated into an original, analytical sentence.

Theme: The main idea or dominant concern of a novel, play, or poem stated in a generalized, abstract way. Example: "Crime does not pay." "Honesty is the best policy."

Tone: The attitude a novel or poem takes toward its subject.

Tragedy: A story in which the character begins at a high point but ends badly, often because of a fatal flaw in his character that causes him to make poor choices. Example: *King Lear* by William Shakespeare; *Oedipus Rex* by Sophocles.

Tragic Flaw: An error in judgment, accidental wrongdoing, or unwitting mistake that results in tragedy, derived from the Greek idea of *hamartia*, or missing the mark.

Tragic Hero: A character, often a noble person of high rank, who comes to a disastrous end in his or her confrontation with a superior force (fortune, the gods, social forces, universal values), but also comes to understand the meaning of his or her deeds and to accept an appropriate punishment.

Unreliable Narrator: A speaker or voice whose narration is consciously or unconsciously deceiving. This type of narration is often subtly undermined by details in the story or through inconsistencies with general knowledge.

Voice: The style, personality, and tone of a narrative; also the speaker or narrator. An appropriate voice captures the correct level of formality, social distance, and personality for the purpose of the writing and the audience.

Writer's Handbook: See *handbook*.

— You will also find the Glossary online: https://excellence-in-literature.com/glossary/

Selected Resources

There is an endless supply of books on reading, writing, and literature, but it can be difficult to find the best. As I look at my bookshelves, I see that many books boast an array of sticky-note flags. When I open them, I find extensive marginal notations, underlined passages, and occasionally, extra slips of paper left at especially important spots. Here are just a few of the most-thumbed volumes on my bookshelves, as well as a few e-resources you will find helpful.

A CiRCE Guide to Reading– This compact guide teaches a multi-layered, flexible approach to reading that includes elements of speed-reading, close reading, and humane reading.

Adventures in Art by David and Shirley Quine- This interactive e-text is designed to help you "visualize the significant changes in ideas throughout history, and then relate those changes to their cultural meaning." This is an excellent art and worldview context supplement to EIL.

American Passages: A Literary Survey- This well-organized site, designed to enhance the study of American literature, offers timelines, art, and other context information in an easily navigated format. One unique feature allows students to construct a multimedia slideshow of selected materials from the site; then use the slideshow for a presentation.

http://www.learner.org/amerpass/index.html

"**Analyzing Poetry**" from Study Guide-

http://www.studyguide.org/poetry_tips.htm

Benét's Reader's Encyclopedia- This wonderful resource is described as "the classic and only encyclopedia of world literature in a single volume including poets, playwrights, novelists, and belletrists, synopses, historical data, major characters, in literature, myths and legends, literary terms, artistic movements, and prize winners." Any of the older editions will include the important elements of the Western literary tradition. I use it often.

The Company of the Creative: A Christian Reader's Guide to Great Literature and Its Themes by David L. Larson- This helpful guide offers brief overviews of great authors and their work, plus useful recommendations for further reading.

Developing Linguistic Patterns Through Poetry Memorization by Andrew Pudewa– To write well, a student needs to internalize the rhythm and cadence of well-composed language. This book will help you accomplish that.

A Dictionary of Literary Symbols by Michael Ferber- This helpful guide, now available free online, "explains . . . literary symbols that we all frequently encounter (such as swan, rose, moon, gold), and gives hundreds of cross-references and quotations" from classic authors, the Bible, and English, American, and European literature.

https://www.academia.edu/people/search?utf8=%E2%9C%93&q=literary+symbols

Discovering Music- Dr. Carol Reynolds has created a "unique curriculum [that] takes you through the history of music, the arts, and Western Culture from 1600 to 1914" in about 13 hours of video instruction. This is an excellent context supplement to EIL. http://discoveringmusic.net/

The Elegant Essay Writing Lessons: Building Blocks for Analytical Writing by Lesha Myers- An elegantly simple introduction to essay writing, organized in units. This may be used before or concurrently with Excellence in Literature.

Excellence-in-Literature.com- Here you will find many of the context resources and study references used in the *Excellence in Literature* curriculum and *Classics-Based Writing*.

Excellence in Literature Handbook for Writers- The first half of this 400+ page handbook for student and teacher contains detailed instruction on essay writing, including a selection of sample outlines for different types of papers. The second half is a guide to usage and style, including sentence construction, word usage, punctuation, and more.

Gutenberg: Free Books- This wonderful site contains many classic books in digital form. I do not recommend reading extensively on the computer screen, but these book files can be useful when you cannot find a copy locally.

How to Read a Book: The Classic Guide to Intelligent Reading by Mortimer J. Adler and Charles Van Doren- There are multiple levels of reading—elementary, inspectional, and synoptical—and the authors clearly explain each and teach the reader how to appropriately read various types of literature.

How to Read and Why by Harold Bloom- A Yale professor and author of many books on literature, Bloom offers this brief volume of selections chosen not "as an exclusive list of what to read, but rather a sampling of works that best illustrate why to read." For a more extensive overview of the classics, you may want to read The Western Canon.

How to Read Literature Like a Professor: A Lively and Entertaining Guide to Reading Between the Lines by Thomas C. Foster- This light-hearted guide offers a very accessible look at the themes and symbols found under the surface in great literature.

How to Read Slowly: Reading for Comprehension by James W. Sire- Sire, the author of the Christian worldview classic, *The Universe Next Door*, has written an excellent, concise introduction (just six chapters!) to reading literature from a worldview perspective.

Imitations in Writing: The Grammar of Poetry by Matt Whiting- This accessible text "focuses on teaching the fundamentals of poetry (figurative language, meter, rhyme, etc.) by means of imitation and review." We found it to be an easy-to-use introduction to poetry.

Invitation to the Classics: A Guide to Books You have Always Wanted to Read by Louise Cowan and Os Guinness- This attractive guide presents a chronological survey of great literature. The purpose of the book is to "introduce the Western literary masterworks in a clear and simple style that is mature in seriousness and tone and Christian in perspective—and in doing so, to help reawaken Western people to the vibrant heritage of these classics that are rich in themselves and in their two-thousand-year relationship to the Christian faith."

Librivox: Free Audio Books- The exciting thing about LibriVox is that you do not have to be content with just the books they offer—you can record and upload your own! The quality of these amateur recordings varies, but the price is right. http://librivox.org/

The Lifetime Reading Plan by Clifton Fadiman- Fadiman offers an overview of the Western canon, with brief discussions about each author and his or her greatest works. His aim is to help the reader "avoid mental bankruptcy" and to "understand something …of our position in space and time …[and] know how we got the ideas by which …we live."

Norton Anthologies: I recommend looking for used copies of the Norton Anthologies at used bookstores, remainder tables, or online, because they contain extremely reliable, high-quality author introductions and their chronological format makes it easy to see the literary context of the works we will study throughout Excellence in Literature. Other anthologies may be useful, but I like the Norton editions because they tend to stick with the classics, especially in older editions. I suggest getting the American, English, World, and Poetry anthologies.

Norton Literature Online- The W. W. Norton sites, home of the renowned Norton Anthologies, offer a wealth of nicely organized context information, a few audio resources, plus a valuable introduction to writing about literature which includes a glossary, flashcards, and quizzes. Highly recommended. Access the StudySpace for the book you need through http://books.wwnorton.com/studyspace/disciplines/literature.aspx?DiscId=7 or go directly to your area of interest.

http://www.wwnorton.com/college/english/literature/OpenSite.htm

American Literature- www.wwnorton.com/college/english/naal7/

British Literature- http://www.wwnorton.com/college/english/nael/

World Literature- http://www.wwnorton.com/college/english/literature/nawol.htm

Writing About Literature: Norton's basic instruction in how to read analytically and write an analytical essay. This resource seems to move regularly. If this link does not work, try doing a web search for "Writing About Literature: Norton," and you may find it.

http://www.wwnorton.com/college/english/litweb10/writing/welcome.aspx

On Writing Well: An Informal Guide to Writing Nonfiction by William Zinsser- There is a good reason that this classic resource just celebrated its thirtieth anniversary with a new edition; it is an excellent model for its subject. Zinsser begins with an overview of writing principles, then moves into detailed discussion of forms and methods. It is a valuable resource for any writer.

The Politically Incorrect Guide to English and American Literature by Elizabeth Kantor, Ph.D. is a delightful romp through selected English language literature. It begins by pointing out that "the greatest English literature is explicitly Christian and celebrates military courage," and goes on to explain why dead white males deserve the respect they have traditionally received. Overall, the book provides a memorable introduction to the ideas that have shaped the literary world, as well as sound recommendations for books you must not miss (most of them are included in the Excellence in Literature series).

Reading Between the Lines: A Christian Guide to Literature by Gene Edward Veith, Jr.- This interesting guide begins with a chapter on the importance of reading, then progresses through the forms, modes, and traditions of literature, with extensive end-notes for each chapter. It is a book that is worth reading and rereading, for each time you do, you will glean new insights.

Teaching the Classics: A Socratic Method for Literary Education by Adam and Missy Andrews (DVDs and manual)- This would be an excellent course to view during middle school, as well as a few times while working through the Excellence in Literature series. The Socratic method of thinking is applicable to other disciplines as well, and can be an enormous help through the high school and college years.

Vocabulary Study: I like Dynamic Literacy's *Word Build* program, which goes beyond the simple study of roots by using "morphology, the study of the units of meaning in words. [Just as] mastery of phonics helps students 'sound out' unfamiliar words; a mastery of morphics helps students 'mean out' unfamiliar words." An alternative is the *Vocabulary from Classical Roots* series, which presents Greek and Latin roots in a series of well-designed lessons.

Write for College: A Student Handbook- Specific instructions on many types of writing, plus a proofreader's guide to grammar, punctuation, and style, and much more. Younger students may prefer *Writer's INC*, which is similar, but for 11th–12th grades and beyond, *Write for College* or the EIL *Handbook for Writers* (referenced earlier) is most useful.

A Writer's Reference by Diana Hacker- I still turn to this brief handbook because of its handy tabbed format and helpful citation guides, including MLA and APA styles. It would be a useful supplement to either of the other suggested guides.

Word Processing Software

If you do not have a full-featured word processing program such as Microsoft Word, I recommend Google's free online suite of applications, including a word processor, spreadsheet program, and other tools. All you need for access to these is a free Google account, available at https://accounts.google.com/SignUp?.

A second option would be to download OpenOffice, a free, open-source suite of office productivity software. It is available at http://www.openoffice.org.

About the Author

Janice Campbell and her husband Donald homeschooled their sons from preschool into early college using a lifestyle of learning approach influenced by Charlotte Mason, classical learning, and the Thomas Jefferson method. Her books and resources reflect Janice's focus on twaddle-free, active learning (she did have boys, after all!).

Janice speaks at conferences nationwide on subjects including literature, writing, homeschool planning, high school records and transcripts, as well as micro-business and multiple streams of income for homeschool families. She graduated *cum laude* from Mary Baldwin College with a B.A. in English and is the author of the *Excellence in Literature* curriculum for grades 8-12, *Transcripts Made Easy*, and *Get a Jump Start on College*, and publisher of a new edition of the 1857 McGuffey Readers with instructions for use with Charlotte Mason methods. She is also Director of the National Association of Independent Writers and Editors (NAIWE).

Whether teaching high school students to love literature or writers and entrepreneurs how to create multiple streams of income, Janice's focus is on lighting lamps so that others can more easily find their way. Her website, www.Everyday-Education .com, offers inspiration, resources, and a free e-newsletter.

Everyday Education Book List

Here is our current book list. You'll always find the most current information and instant ordering, as well as e-books and new items, at www.Everyday-Education.com, but this will give you an idea of what is currently available.

Books we offer at Everyday-Education.com
Excellence in Literature: Reading and Writing though the Classics—Grades 8-12
English I: *Introduction to Literature*
English II: *Lit & Composition*
English III: *American Literature*
English IV: *British Literature*
English V: *World Literature*
—**Complete Curriculum** (1-5 in books or a binder)
Handbook for Writers (Reference book for high school and college)
TimeFrame: The Twaddle-Free Timeline
Model-Based Writing—coming soon!
1857 McGuffey Readers with Charlotte Mason Instructions
First Reader
Second Reader
Third Reader
Fourth Reader
Fifth Reader
Sixth Reader
— SAVE! Set of Readers 1, 2, and 3 OR Set of Readers 4, 5, and 6
—SAVE! Set of all six Readers
Peaceful Planning Booklets
12- Year Planner: A DIY Scope and Sequence for Peaceful Planning
K-8 Student Record
High School Student Record
Lifetime Reading List
Other good stuff
Transcripts Made Easy
Get a Jump Start on College
Perfect Reading, Beautiful Handwriting
CursiveLogic Workbook and cursive art workbook practice set
Elegant Essay by Lesha Myers: Teacher's Manual and Student Book
Elegant Essay: Student Book only
Evaluate Writing the Easy Way

Books we offer at Everyday-Education.com
Working it Out: Poetry Analysis and Devotional with George Herbert
The Living Page: Charlotte Mason Notebooking
French-Ruled Composition Notebooks for handwriting practice
Microbusiness Curriculum by Carol Topp, CPA– 4 Books
Chenier's *Practical Math Dictionary* and *Application Guide*

IF YOU HAVE NEVER SAID "EXCUSE ME"
TO A PARKING METER
OR BASHED YOUR SHINS ON A FIREPLUG,
YOU ARE PROBABLY WASTING TOO MUCH
VALUABLE READING TIME.

Sherri Chasin Calvo

Made in the USA
Monee, IL
14 December 2019